LET'S KILL 'EM

Understanding and Controlling Violence in Sports

JON LEIZMAN, PH.D.

University Press of America, Inc.
Lanham • New York • Oxford

Copyright © 1999 by
University Press of America,® Inc.
4720 Boston Way
Lanham, Maryland 20706

12 Hid's Copse Rd.
Cumnor Hill, Oxford OX2 9JJ

Library of Congress Cataloging-in-Publication Data

Leizman, Jon.
Let's kill 'em : understanding and controlling violence in sports / Jon
Leizman.
p.   cm.
Includes bibliographical references and index.
1. Violence in sports. 2. Violence in sports—United States—
Prevention. 3. Spectator control—United States. I. Title. II. Title:
Let's kill them.
GV706.7.L44 1999 796'.0973—dc21   99—14399 CIP

ISBN 0-7618-1377-2 (cloth: alk. ppr.)
ISBN 0-7618-1378-0 (pbk: alk. ppr.)

∞™ The paper used in this publication meets the minimum
requirements of American National Standard for Information
Sciences—Permanence of Paper for Printed Library Materials,
ANSI Z39.48—1984

Dedication

For Lydia.

Contents

Preface

This book explores how the traditional Western ways of approaching competition have distorted the manner in which we teach and learn how to compete, and it suggests ways to control the violence in professional team sports. In addition to elucidating several practical measures that professional sports can take to control violence, this study offers an extended discussion of an important aspect of the problem of violence in sport: how we understand competition in terms of our focus toward our opponent and toward ourselves. Among the most important suggested administrative and legal remedies to control excess violence in professional team sports is that both the athletes and the team's ownership should be held legally and financially accountable for any intentional, beyond the rules injuries inflicted on an opponent. Furthermore, a new paradigm for professional sports and for sport training needs to be established, one that adopts an attitude that emphasizes the unity of mind, body, and spirit. The martial arts of T'ai Chi Chuan and Aikido present a model for developing such a training attitude.

Acknowledgments

I would like to thank Ed Wingard, Gary Andrews, Ralph Schoenfeld, Deborah Cattin, Ken Bennet, and especially Bethe Hagens.

Introduction

I start with five fundamental suppositions. First, I assume the intrinsic value of team sports on all levels—from elementary school to college to professional levels. That is, I am in no way suggesting that programs or sports be curtailed because of what I call excess, unnecessary violence. Rather, ways need to be found to increase the value of team sports, both to participants and to spectators, by reducing violence that distracts from the positive, competitive essence of the game.

Second, it is my assumption that values and ethics greatly affect the tenor of an individual's participation in, and perception of, sport, particularly team sports. While Charles Barkley or Daryl Strawberry, for instance, may disclaim that they are "role models" while trying to sell shoes for Nike or Reebok, their expressed way of competing (and living) communicates and underlines the societal values that children begin learning as soon as their parents turn on the television to the Houston Rockets/Chicago Bulls game or to ESPN while it is reporting on Strawberry's tax evasion sentencing, spousal abuse arrest, or cocaine possession charges.

Third, I assume that the role models that professional athletes currently present often result in an increasing level of unnecessary violence in team sports at younger age levels, due in part to increased television exposure. Of course, televised sports violence has been around since television, and brawls have happened since the advent of team sport, but people's access to sport, via television and an ever-increasing number of teams in all sports, have exaggerated at least the perception of the problem, and perhaps the problem itself.

Fourth, I assume that this increasing tendency toward unnecessary violence in sport can, and should, be reversed. This is in agreement with the administrators of professional sport who have tried, with limited success, to curb the unnecessary violence through such measures as increased fines and suspensions.

Fifth, I assume that there is a vital distinction between aggression in sport and unnecessary violence in sport. That is, aggression is a result of the natural focusing of inner competitive energies while violence is a displaced expression of those energies in that it dilutes the focus by projecting energy in ways that detract from an athlete's competitive performance. In other words, violence often attempts to replace skillful competition.

This book follows an essentially heuristic approach. That is, I explore the philosophical and psychological underpinnings of violence in professional sports, and I develop a case for a speculative formulation: that a combination of administrative and educational efforts can help stem the rising tide of unnecessary and excessive violence in professional sports.

The specific approach taken in this book follows along one of the major lines of contemporary sports philosophy. That is, Wertz (1991) identifies three trends which have emerged in sports philosophy, and in philosophy in general, in the 20th century. First, there is "the speculative tradition" which focuses on "the metaphysical problems of sport." Second, there is "the existential/phenomenological tradition." As Wertz sees it, "instead of raising questions concerning the essence of sport, these writers try to portray what human existence in sport is like from the standpoint of human subjectivity, i.e., of the experiencing subject." Third, there is an "analytic tradition" that "attempts an analysis of sport ideas; for examples, the ideas of a well-played game and sportsmanship."[1]

This book focuses on the first of Wertz's categories, the metaphysical tradition, and on examining three essential hypotheses, namely:

1. American sport, particularly at the professional, major team sport level, is unacceptably violent, especially in terms of the ethical values such violence teaches younger sport participants.

2. Administrative remedies to on-the-field, court, or rink violence must be strengthened, and some of the most recent rules changes suggest more effective means by which excessive violence in professional sports can be curtailed.

3. The values of Eastern, internally-directed ways of thinking about sport can help diminish the level of excessive violence by re-directing sport's natural aggression from an emphasis on punishing one's opponent to an emphasis on intensifying one's internal focus and improving one's athletic performance.

The focus of the study is also on elucidating a philosophy of sport that overcomes some of the intrinsic limitations of our culture's dominant perspective on competition. That is, I first discuss, via a history of the philosophy of Western sport since the ancient Greeks, the cultural antecedents for our current dilemmas about sports violence. Second, I outline the deficiencies and inadequacies of the current situations as to the administrative remedies for excessive violence in the major American team sports. Third, I develop an overview of sport that includes several concepts grafted from "Eastern" philosophical traditions, principally from Taoism and Zen Buddhism. Finally, I suggest several philosophical and administrative remedies for the plague of outside-the-game, on-the-field (or court or rink) violence that, like many diseases, strikes hardest at the youngest and most vulnerable among us.

Notes to Introduction

1. Spencer K. Wertz, *Talking a Good Game: Inquiries into the Principles of Sport* (Dallas: Southern Methodist University Press, 1991), pp. 23-25.

Chapter 1

ℬℭ

An Overview of Violence in Sports

Introduction

Like an epidemic against which no vaccine has yet been developed, violence spreads from one person to another, sparing neither adult nor child, creating distress and pain for each of its victims. Unlike many diseases, however, there is no immunity conferred once a person recovers from his or her first exposure. In his perceptive article, "Way Out of Control," *Sports Illustrated* writer, Jack McCallum, relates a brief discussion between a friend of his and the friend's son that took place on their way to a baseball game. Here, the subtle, invisible spread of the infection of violence can be heard clearly.

> "' Jeez, Dad,' the boy said, 'I hope we see one today. I've never seen one.'
> 'A homer?' says the dad.
> 'No,' says the kid. 'A brawl.'"[1]

Of course, the problem of violence in our society is not limited to professional sports, nor is the need to understand the genesis of violence intrinsically different when studying sports than when studying other sometimes violent aspects of our culture. Nevertheless, sports in general, and professional team sports in particular, provide a highly visible arena for studying the phenomenon of violence and for developing methods of removing that violence. Indeed, this book's working definition of violence is simply "behavior which causes harm, occurs outside of the rules of the sport, and is unrelated to the competitive objectives of the sport."[2]

Our society is rife with violence, and our societal attitudes toward competition and toward violent aggression in "the real world" greatly affect our attitude toward competition and violent aggression within sport. Too often, it is the worst aspects of anti-social, violent aggression that are emphasized in competitive sports, from the youngest level to the professional ranks. As Thomas Tutko and William Bruns presciently wrote in the mid-1970s:

> . . . Parents or coaches might argue, 'Look, you're talking about pro-
> fessional sports—but the pros have nothing to do with us.' I strongly
> disagree. In my opinion, the professionals (and many of their collegiate
> counterparts) are becoming an increasingly destructive model for
> childhood sports, from coaching styles to the competitive ethos, and if
> left unchecked, this madness will eventually undermine the inherent
> values of organized sports.[3]

In the past decade and a half, since Tutko and Bruns published their book, the "destructive model" they speak of has been left largely unchecked, although some recent efforts by the National Basketball Association (NBA) and the National Hockey League (NHL) are beginning to demonstrate that administrative remedies at least can be partially successful as a tool to lessen violence in professional team sports. However, despite periodic administrative efforts to curb overt, beyond the rules violence, especially in professional sports, melees are as common as ever in baseball and football, and the values that sport explicitly and implicitly teach have become distorted.

Leonard Coleman, Jr., baseball's National League President, echoed the sentiment that how professional athletes behave on the field affects young sportsmen and women. When asked by *USA Today* columnist, Hal Bodley, if he thought the increased level of violence was good for the game, then newly appointed President Coleman replied that he intended to put a stop to brawls because "it's not good for baseball . . . [and] it's just a matter of time before somebody is seriously hurt." He went on to note that "another very important reason for discouraging it to the extent of my powers is that kids emulate major league ballplayers. I've got millions of kids watching this game around the country and baseball players are role models. I don't want kids in Little League games . . . emulating them."

Bodley also told a brief, revealing story of a colleague who had related what one of the Little Leaguers he coaches said on the way to a recent game: "When one of the youngsters mentioned he hoped he wouldn't get 'beaned' by a pitch, another looked up at the coach . . . and asked, 'I'm not sure. When exactly are you supposed to charge the mound' ?"[4]

Do we want to be training Little Leaguers to punch out the pitcher in retaliation for getting hit by a baseball? Do we want to teach young basketball players that trash talking is acceptable and that wrestling your opponent to the court, as New York Knick, Derek Harper, did to Chicago Bull, Jo Jo English, on national television, virtually at the feet of NBA Commissioner, David Stern, is to be tolerated?

The answer to these somewhat rhetorical questions is a resounding " no!" for many people affiliated with sports administration. Unfortunately, how to go about making the necessary changes to insure that on the court, playing field, and rink violence is curbed is not so clear to these same administrators. Is it simply that "we have overpaid and over-publicized giants on an ego trip," as George Vecsey suggests?[5] Or can the violence be controlled merely by enforcing tough new rules, along the lines of the NHL's guidelines enacted after the brawl-filled 1986-87 season, rules that allow for long, unpaid suspensions for players and coaches? Or are there additional ways of handling violence that can help diminish its levels, perhaps ways that involve rethinking how we encourage athletes to look at competition?

These questions and considerations prompted me to study various ways of limiting violence in professional sports. Thus, this book grows from my heart-felt concern that more effective and inventive means are needed to control professional sports violence.

The Problem

American professional sport has failed to control competitive violence, and alternative approaches to the problem of violence in professional sport are needed if this situation is to be controlled or even reversed. Since cable television has greatly expanded the exposure of major professional sports, this issue has increasingly come to the fore. Further, despite occasionally significant efforts in recent years to control unacceptable violence through more vigorous administrative enforcement of existing rules in all major professional sports, the level and frequency of violence has not been effectively curbed. Indeed, as was evident in both baseball and basketball in the spring of 1994, the level and severity of brawling is disturbing. While a certain amount of this may be due to the manner in which television and print journalists cover sport, there is a great deal of room for constructive change in how professional athletes manifest their natural competitive aggression.

It is thus my contention that American sport, particularly at the professional, major team sport level, has become unacceptably violent, particularly in terms of the ethical values such violence implicitly teaches younger sport participants at the collegiate, high school, and even elementary school levels. This book discusses three possible approaches to controlling the problem of violence in professional sports.

One aspect of the problem lies in how our culture has learned to conceptualize competition and violence in human nature and in sports. The roots of this violence lie deep in the soil of our culture's history. From Western culture's earliest written records, competition and violence have been linked in a way that they have not been in many other cultures.

Among the most important aspects of this discussion is the genesis of the Western notions of the "body/mind" division, a distinction that generally is not made in other cultural traditions. From Plato through the early Christian theologians, Saint Augustine and Thomas Aquinas, and then through the philosophies of Descartes, Schopenhauer, and Freud, the dualistic philosophy of Western culture augments the military origin of many sports to create an implicit philosophy of sport that rather easily incorporates violence into its ethos.

The second of these three approaches concerns developing and enforcing more effective administrative procedures directed at minimizing the problem of violence in sports. Since recent changes in some rules in both hockey and basketball seem to be having a positive effect on controlling unacceptable levels of violence in those sports, perhaps additional administrative changes and actions can augment the present efforts.

The third aspect of this book's discussion about controlling violence in professional sports involves an exploration of the values of Eastern, internally directed, ways of thinking. This approach can potentially help diminish the level of violence by re-directing sport's natural aggression from an emphasis on punishing one's opponent to an emphasis on intensifying one's internal focus and improving one's athletic performance. That is, by over-emphasizing beating an opponent, traditional Western ways of approaching competition have distorted the manner in which we teach and learn how to compete. Eastern approaches to sport offer an alternative way of thinking that can simultaneously curb excess violence and improve an individual's performance. By focusing one's competitive concentration on achieving the best individual and team performance rather than on "fighting an enemy," it is possible to maximize one's athletic potential by eliminating the energy drains of incidental factors. Moreover, the Eastern approach of redirecting the energy from an attack ultimately conserves energy, giving the attacked individual a subtle tactical and energetic advantage.

Significance

There may be several ways that sport psychologists, administrators, and participants can help control and, ultimately, greatly reduce the level of unnecessary violence in the major team sports of football, baseball, basketball, and hockey. Certainly, most responsible athletic program administrators agree that there is an increasing amount of such violence and that this it is not a good thing. All the professional leagues have made widely-publicized attempts to handle excess violence in their own sports, though the effectiveness of their approaches has been incomplete. There is no commonly held agreement as to what can, and should, be done to alter the *status quo* for the better.

The significance of this book lies in its offering a partial solution to one aspect of the problem of violence in sport: how we understand competition in terms of our focus toward our opponent and toward ourselves. That is, traditional Western ways of approaching competition have distorted the manner in which we teach and learn how to compete by over-emphasizing beating an opponent. Unfortunately, the Vince Lombardi school of thought—"Winning isn't everything. It's the only thing"—is still the dominant thinking of major team sports in America. Eastern approaches to sport offer an alternative way of thinking that can simultaneously curb excess violence and improve an individual's performance. By focusing one's competitive concentration on achieving the best individual and team performance rather than on "fighting an enemy," it is possible to maximize one's athletic potential by eliminating the energy drains of incidental factors.

Notes

1. Jack McCallum, "Way Out Of Control," *Sports Illustrated*, May 23, 1994, p. 28.
2. Peter C. Terry and John J. Jackson, "The Determinants and Control of Violence in Sport." *Quest*, v. 37, 1985, pp. 27-37.
3. Thomas Tutko and William Bruns, *Winning Is Everything and Other American Myths* (New York: Macmillan, 1976), p. 46.
4. Hal Bodley, "NL Boss Takes Hard Line on Outbreak of Brawling." *USA Today*, May 6, 1994, p. 6C.
5. George Vecsey, "Basketball Hulksters Concentrate on Business." *The New York Times*, May 16, 1994, p. C4.

Chapter 2

🕮

Sports Literature

The literature of the philosophy of sport includes quite a number of articles and portions of books that focus on various aspects of competition. In addition to articles in professional journals, such as the *Journal of the Philosophy of Sport*, popular magazines (e.g., *Sports Illustrated*, *Sport*) and newspapers (e.g., *The New York Times*, *USA Today*) frequently run articles and opinion pieces about violence and competition in sport.

My approach to this review of literature is partly chronological and partly according to genres (e.g., books, professional journal articles, popular press writing). I begin with a look at the literature up until the late 1960s, before many academics considered the philosophy of sport to be a worthy area of inquiry, concentrating on the ancient Greek philosophers whose writings are at the headwaters of Western recorded culture. Second, I look at collections of essays about the philosophy of sport, published from the 1960s to the present, that chronicle the changing nature of how American society and sport philosophers view issues of violence and competition. Third, I mention a number of journalistic articles, both in professional journals and in popular magazines and newspapers. Fourth, I consider several book length studies by a single author that present important landmarks in the development of the philosophy of sport. Fifth, I address those authors, such as Timothy Gallwey, and Huang and Lynch, who have presented what they call the "inner game" of sports. These writers focus on defining a new paradigm for competition that emphasizes how and why the "inner game" can provide a guidepost on the road away from uncurbed violence in sport.

Greece to the 1960s

It is worth noting that, in the culture of ancient Greece, sport and the military were inextricably linked. As Desmond Lee states, Plato "makes it clear that he is thinking of a military as much as of an athletic training" when he addresses issues of sport and physical education.[1] Moreover, Plato viewed both physical and literary training as aimed at the development of character. In Plato's view, a person who developed only the physical side of his personality, avoiding the intellectual and literary side, "becomes an unintelligent philistine with . . . an animal addiction to settle everything by brute force."[2]

There are several excellent books that deal with Greek and Roman athletics. Two of the best of these are by the British writer, H.A. Harris: *Greek Athletes and Athletics* (1966) and *Sport in Greece and Rome* (1972). Of course, quite a bit of the ancient world's attitude toward sport can be discerned from such literary sources as Homer's *The Iliad*, where the funeral of the Greek warrior, Patroclos, is the occasion for sports competition.

Few philosophers in the two and a half millennia between Plato and the twentieth century wrote at all extensively of organized athletics, let alone professional athletics, for the play of such endeavors on the canvas of society was too limited to attract serious critical attention. Nevertheless, in some works of literature, we can see implicit commentaries on the infancy of American professional sport. In at least one case, violence and team sport are directly connected: Mark Twain, in his 1889 novel, *A Connecticut Yankee in King Arthur's Court*, makes this a satirical and humorous connection. Bringing true civilization to medieval Great Britain, in Twain's parody of late nineteenth century America, meant creating baseball "to furnish an escape for the extra steam of chivalry." Of course, as is still true today (fortunately, to a slightly lesser extent), umpires had a particularly hard and undeserved time of it:

Of course, I couldn't get these people to leave off their armor; they wouldn't do that when they bathed . . . When a man was running, and threw himself on his stomach, it was like an ironclad coming into port. At first I appointed men of no rank to act as umpires, but I had to discontinue that . . . The umpire's first decision was usually his last; they broke him in two with a bat, and his friends toted him home on a shutter. When it was noticed that no umpire ever survived a game, umpiring got to be unpopular. So I was obliged to appoint somebody whose rank and lofty position under the government would protect him.[3]

In the first decade of the twentieth century, an Englishman, L. Graves, advanced "the first modern thesis concerning sport."[4] For Graves, coming out of Victorian England and its Etonian sense of ethics, there was a clear distinction between competition as recreation and competition as sport. In no way, according to this quaintly out-moded view, could or should professional sport have anything to do with sensible competition:

In so far as a pursuit is followed as a means of livelihood it ceases to be sport, and becomes merely a matter of business. Sport is followed for no other end than to afford pleasure to those participating in it, and a sportsman follows sport for no other reason than to enjoy that pleasure . . . Once the idea is imported into sport that a man's subsistence depends upon it, then the pleasantness of sport as recreation ceases, and we import into it the bitterness of the world's struggle for existence. There are things which a man will do when his back is against the wall, and he feels that his own livelihood or that of his wife and children are dependent upon him, which he would not dream of doing if this feeling were removed.[5]

Such a view of competition, while it is obviously antiquated, does contain a kernel of continuing wisdom: pursuing sport for money, whether simply for a livelihood or to make the millions now paid to top athletes, does alter the equation and makes sport into an enterprise closer to the mainstream of human activity. That Graves was uncomfortable with this association of occupation and sport is certainly attributable, in part, to his own upper class background and predilections. But the past century has proven, if nothing else about sport, that sport faces the same challenges as other areas of human endeavor, and that making a living at sport in the age of television is not intrinsically different than making a living as a teacher or tradesman. Without doubt, Graves' approach to sport separates it unnaturally from other endeavors.

Kenneth Schmitz, in the late 1950s, elaborated upon, and somewhat updated, Graves' approach to sport. In his essay "Sports and Play; Suspension of the Ordinary," he rues the increasingly important relationship between sport and business, maintaining that professional sport includes a binding force foreign to "the game itself." This binding force:

> . . . does not lie in interest in the game itself but rather is . . . ultimately enforced by values not intrinsic to the game. Perhaps the dearest distinction is between the wage the pro earns and the win or loss of the game. Win or lose, for a time at least he is paid a wage for services delivered; but he gets a victory only when 'the gods of the game' smile upon him. Play ceases when the primary reasons for undertaking it are alien to the values of the play world itself.[6]

Schmitz goes on to characterize professional motives in a more generous way than had Graves ("these motives are not unworthy; they are simply not motives of play"), but his evident distaste for connecting sport and professionalism perhaps unwittingly makes him the mid-century inheritor of Graves' Etonian-bred sport elitism.

Warren Fraleigh, writing in the early 1980s, also reflects the point of view that the "rules of the game" prohibit certain kinds of unsportsmanlike behavior, even though such behavior is commonly practiced under the guise of "the good foul." In a rather naive approach, Fraleigh maintains that:

> . . . intentional violation of the rules done for the purpose of achieving an end otherwise difficult to achieve, but performed in such a way that the violator expects to receive and willingly accepts the penalty, detracts from the good sports contest. Although such intentional violations, of which the 'good' foul in basketball is used as one illustration, are 'good' in terms of the rational self-interest of the violator, they are not good in terms of the good sports contest.[7]

Among the most useful books in tracing some of Western history's violent tendencies in sport is Coe, Teasdale, and Wickham's 1992 book, *More Than a Game*. Their chapter on "the violent tendency," is particularly useful, although the book concentrates on such non-American sports as soccer and rugby and non-team sports such as boxing.

The most popular form in which philosophy of sport has addressed issues such as competition has been via essays rather than in the form of book-length studies by a single author. In the following two sections, I look at book-length collections of essays and at essays from professional journals and from the popular press.

Book-Length Collections of Essays

Several of the collections of essays that can be classified under the rubric of philosophy of sport were originally done in the context of sociology. In general, the collections that emphasize sociology look at how sports and society interact in Western culture, whereas the collections that emphasize a philosophical approach focus on the role of an athlete or on developing an overview, ideal, or paradigm of competition. However, at times it is difficult to separate the literature about the sociology of sport from that of the philosophy of sport, and in volumes such as *Sport and American Society*, (1970) edited by George Sage, and *Sport, Culture, and Society*, (1969) edited by John Loy and Gerald Kenyon, several articles overlap into philosophical approaches.

In Sage's volume, the section on "Sport and American Education" touches on several points that have been taken up by philosophy of sport in the past twenty years. However, from the point of view of the present, the conclusions the contributors to this book sometimes reach seem almost as outdated as Graves' opinions do. For instance, in the article "Consequences of Participation in Interscholastic Sports: A Review and Prospectus," the authors maintain that, "it is possible that a national sports movement might enhance certain government efforts toward social change [and] reduce certain traditional hostilities based on social and geographic origins."[8] While it is true that athletics have had a function in reducing the most overt "traditional hostilities," including racial hostilities, the nature of competition has become personalized in a way that often undermines government efforts to encourage positive social changes. In other words, at times it seems that the traditional hostilities, based on factors such as race, have been replaced by a sense of increased, personalized, and unnecessary violence on the playing field, as an echo of the transformation our entire society has been undergoing since this book's publication. On the other hand, Mr. Sage himself, in an article in his book titled "Humanism in Sport," points more accurately toward the direction of competition as a means of self-actualization rather than as merely triumphing over an opponent or obeying the dictates of a coach. As Sage puts it:

The end of sport is the joy, exhilaration, and self-fulfillment that one obtains from movement; it is the display of skill, the challenge of matching tactical wits with competitors, and the sensual feelings that arise in competition. Using victory as the only end, the goal of sport competition is too limiting, confining . . . short-sighted . . . One reason winning is so overvalued is that we haven't been taught to enjoy the doing—the process—of whatever it is we are attempting.[9]

Here, the idea that self-fulfillment is the goal of competition is worth noting, for this train of thought is elaborated upon in a number of later books and articles.

Furthermore, the complexity of the relationship between sport and the rest of society was starting to be explored by the late 1960s, and the dictums of Graves and Schmitz that professional sport and competition represented an untenable combination were fading. As David Riesman and Reuel Denney wrote in Loy and Kenyon's volume, *Sport, Culture, and Society*: "In the American culture as a whole, no sharp line exists between work and play, and in some respects the more work-like an activity becomes, the more it can successfully conceal elements of playfulness."[10]

Of more direct importance to the philosophy of sport is Robert Osterhoudt's 1973 volume of essays, *The Philosophy of Sport: A Collection of Original Essays*. Osterhoudt (who later helped found, and served as Editor-in-Chief, of *The Journal of the Philosophy of Sport*) includes a section of essays on "The Ethical Status of Sport" that directly discusses issues relevant to the heart of athletics as a competitive endeavor. Specifically, the debate is between James Keating, a strong proponent of the idea that competitive struggle is always outwardly-directed, "an attempt . . . to get or keep any thing . . . to the exclusion of others or in greater measure than others," and William Sadler, who holds that such a view of athletics is "detrimental to the realization of full humanness."[11]

Another volume which contains a number of pertinent essays comes from a Canadian source (The Canadian Scholars' Press)—*Philosophy of Sport and Physical Activity*, edited by Pasquale Galasso. The essays concerning how we look at competition are particularly noteworthy here, including Saul Ross's "Winning and Losing in Sport: A Radical Reassessment."

Essays in Professional Journals and the Popular Press

The principal sport philosophy publication during the 1970s and 1980s was *The Journal of the Philosophy of Sport*. In this journal, the debate about the essentials of competition intensified, and all sides of an issue were generally presented, with articles and responses to articles appearing in the same, or subsequent, issues. In virtually all of its issues, it dealt to one degree or another with the debate about modes of competition, and the following discussion of articles that appeared in this publication is a selection rather than a comprehensive assessment of each relevant article.

The 1978 issue, for instance, contains an article by Drew Hyland, "Competition and Friendship," that underscores the then-emerging point of view that antagonistic competition obscures a vital element of cooperation between competitors. "Competitive play," he writes, "should be one of those occasions where our encounters, intense, immediate, and total, are those of friendship, in which we attain to a fulfillment, however momentary, together."[12]

In the next year's (1979) annual issue, this journal featured an article, "Towards a Western Philosophy of the Eastern Martial Arts," aimed at debunking what the authors thought to be unfounded claims of the martial arts as leading to "the formation of good, moral, character; to nonviolent attitudes and behavior; and . . . to enlightenment, or to some sort of mystic consciousness or divine union."[13] This article was partly in response to articles in previous issues, notably the 1977 issue, volume IV, to which Spencer K. Wertz contributed "Zen, Yoga, and Sports: Eastern Philosophy for Western Athletes."[14]

Several years later, in 1986 and 1987, the *Journal of the Philosophy of Sport* printed articles by Shinobu Abe that add to the discussion of how Eastern ways of viewing competition can be successfully grafted into Western athletics. In Zen philosophy, "body and mind are integrated as an action of the Self."[15] Abe outlines the Zen philosophy of sport first developed in the philosophy of Kitaro Nishida (1870-1945). At its heart, Nishida's view incorporates Zen principles of the unity of mind, body, and spirit:

> When we become eye and ear with our entire being, feeling passes over into things and is naturally accompanied by the flow of aesthetic emotion as expression . . . . We must proceed from a profound consideration of the relationship between spirit and body. In the

standpoint of absolute will, there is no distinction between the interior
and exterior of the mind. There is only activity of mind and body as
one lived reality.[16]

As is discussed in Chapter 5, the philosophy that there is no distinction
between "the interior and exterior of the mind" is in agreement with the
holographic model of the nature of reality developed by Pribham, Bohm,
Talbot, and others.

In the past several years, sports journalists also have been prominent
among those proposing new rules to control violence in professional
sports. Indeed, in the past two years (1993-95) there has been a journalistic
outcry against the increasing violence in basketball and baseball,
particularly. Hal Bodley of *USA Today*, George Vecsey and Harvey
Araton of the *New York Times*, and Jack McCallum of *Sports Illustrated*
have all published pointed articles that urge the major professional sports
to better police themselves when it comes to unnecessary violence.

For a number of years, *Sports Illustrated* has led the call for more
and stronger administrative remedies for violence in team sports, and
every couple of months, they offer new ideas. For instance, in addition
to Jack McCallum's excellent article about baseball brawls, "Way Out of
Control," Peter King's article in the December 19, 1994, issue, "Halt
the Head Hunting," is well worth attention. King decries the
"unprecedented viciousness" in football which has led to "premature
retirement" of several players.[17]

Moreover, newspapers across the country have editorialized about
violence in sport, and many local sports columnists have added their
voices to calls for stricter rules, greater enforcement of existing rules,
and increased attention to the physical and emotional toll violence takes
on the players. Many of these writers give fans their only dose of the
harsh reality behind the injuries of their favorite sports heroes, for it is in
the local daily newspapers (and, of course, on ESPN) that most of America
gets its sports news. For example, Mike Preston, a *Baltimore Sun* staff
writer, authored a terrifically informative piece, "The Breaks of the
Game," for the December 28, 1994, issue. In this article, Preston
chronicles several former pro football players' lives of pain, and he quotes
the director of benefits of the NFL Player's Association, Miki Yaras-
Davis, about the physical condition of retired players: "You ever go to
a retired players association convention? . . . It's an orthopedic surgeon's
dream. They all have the crablike walk, and it's hard to believe they
were once these feared gladiators. Forty-year-old players are having the

same problems as 80-year-old men."[18]   While the tone is often less philosophically authoritative than the predominant tone of professional journals or scholarly studies, a great deal of deeply personal testimonial and documentary evidence is contained in these articles.

Book-Length Studies

Of the writers who have produced book-length studies in the field of philosophy of sport, none is more widely recognized than Paul Weiss as a founder of the discipline.

The social and political turmoil of the 1960s spilled over into all areas of American culture, including sport. Of course, professional sport had, by the 1960s, begun to assume the iconic status it currently possesses. A few of the serious commentators on sport still echoed Graves' and Schmitz's belief that professionalism diluted the value of sport, but alternative approaches to issues of competition also started to emerge, sometimes from unanticipated directions.

Weiss, in his important 1969 book, *Sport: A Philosophic Inquiry*, retains a strong measure of the old Etonian ethic, even while attempting to expand the recognition of the philosophy of sport as a legitimate field of academic study. "The athlete's world is set over against the everyday world," Weiss maintained. "Economic demands and the satisfaction of appetites are for the moment put aside." Weiss acknowledges that, like other "ethical men in their endeavors to realize ideal goals,"[19] professionals are not a *priori* anathema to the concept of competition in true "sport." Moreover, even though Weiss is in the Western, Platonic tradition in separating the mind and the body, his book helped open up the field of philosophy of sport so that, only a few years later, the literature of the field began burgeoning.

Sport: A Philosophic Inquiry, presents a series of metaphysical speculations about sport. As Wertz notes, Weiss is in the speculative tradition of philosophy, and his interest is in such areas as sport "as a solution to the problem of the one and the many, and in the nature of a team. His works are attempts to locate sport within the dimension of societal reality."[20] Although Weiss may not speak to some of the issues of professional sport, he deserves a good deal of credit for beginning the academic dialogue that connects sport with philosophy, a dialogue that was picked up in an altered form by several later writers.

One of the most published writers in the philosophy of sport field is Earle F. Ziegler. Ziegler is particularly keen to fit sport into the mainstream of philosophy of education, and he has undoubtedly been a force in doing this for the past quarter century. Unfortunately, his thinking is rather conventional and offers little in the way of creating a viable paradigm for a less violent, more effective competitive attitude. That is, although he recognizes the need to see professional athletes as legitimate sportsmen and women, his solution is to create a new category called "semiprofessionals."[21] Moreover, he is mostly concerned with how professional athletes deport themselves in the sense of controlling their behavior in order to be better role models. He advocates that "professional athletes . . . devote their lives to a social ideal . . . whose later life aim is to serve others through sport."[22]

Several other books, both academic and popular, have attempted to grapple with issues involving competition and ethics in sport, including Vanderzwaag's academic 1972 book, *Toward a Philosophy of Sport*,[23] and Glenn Dickey's amusingly popular 1974 book, *The Jock Empire*. Dickey does speak clearly about the growing acceptance of professional athletics as legitimate sportsmen and women, the turn of the century Etonian ethics, by 1974, having gone the way of horse-drawn carriages and gas street lamps: "Present-day athletes are true professionals and very interested in the size of their paychecks. That is not to say that they don't enjoy playing, or that they do not play their best."[24]

One book worthy of special note is Don Atyeo's *Blood & Guts: Violence in Sports*. Atyeo, an Australian journalist, takes a journey through the dark side of sport, from its violent genesis from hunting and war games, to the relatively sophisticated violence of modern team sports. In the process, he spans the globe, giving historical and anecdotal evidence of how brutal some of our human pastimes have become. Nor does Atyeo spare fans from his sharply critical pen: "To anyone who has kept half an eye cocked on sport . . . it should be blindingly obvious that sporting competition involving . . . violence, leads to spectator aggression on a depressingly frequent number of occasions."[25]

Spectator aggression also figures heavily into John Underwood's excellent 1984 volume, *Spoiled Sport: A Fan's Notes on the Troubles of Spectator Sports*. In his chapter entitled "Violence Unleashed," Underwood discusses a number of current issues and offers some intriguing legal and administrative solutions to violence, including holding the offending player's club responsible when injuries occur.[26] These issues, and Underwood's contribution to the discussion, are reviewed in some depth in Chapter 4 of this book.

A New Paradigm for Competition

The new paradigm for competition that was partly an outgrowth of the societal turmoil of the late 1960s spawned a number of books from the mid-1970s on, books that included elements that previously were missing in western conceptions of sport. That is, among the elements of the 1960s that gradually filtered down to all levels of culture was an increased interest in alternative approaches to visualizing and living one's life. Many of these alternatives were loosely borrowed and adapted from Eastern metaphysical and philosophical models, including the meditational model of Zen Buddhism. Following are reviews of several books that deal directly, in whole or in part, with developing a new, and more effective, competitive paradigm. This new paradigm, rather than being "Eastern" or "Western" includes important elements of both traditional types of approaches.

In 1974, George Leonard, a psychologist who has written extensively in a number of fields, including sports psychology, proposed a recipe for what he called "The Ultimate Athlete." In his book of that title, he spoke extensively of the need to infuse Western sport with the spirit of Aikido, the Japanese art of self-defense. Leonard's first Aikido teacher, Robert Nadeau, described himself as "basically a meditation teacher":

> Nadeau explained that competition is forbidden in Aikido. Competition is limiting. Furthermore, it is not the way the universe operates. We would learn by cooperating, not competing, with each other. 'Aikido's spirit,' according to Master Uyeshiba, 'is that of loving attack and that of peaceful reconciliation.'[27]

The notion of "loving attack and peaceful reconciliation" is far from the dominant paradigm of professional athletics today. But, as several other authors have pointed out since Leonard's observations, going in this direction might be of great help in getting even professional athletes to maximize their skills.

The martial arts also provide a great deal of material of direct interest for this book. Among the most informative of books is one called *Aikido: The Way of Harmony*, by John Stevens and Shirata Rinjiro which gives a clear sense of the history and philosophy of Aikido. Several other books on Aikido and T'ai Chi Ch'uan, including Tem Horwitz, Susan Kimmelman, and H.H. Lui's *T'ai Chi Ch'uan: The Technique of Power*, provide background information on the philosophy of contemporary martial arts.

Another quite useful text in elucidating the new paradigm of competition is *Mind over Matter: Higher Martial Arts* by Shi Ming and Siao Weijia. This book explores the Chinese science of the mind/body relationship, as well as the refinement of consciousness through the martial arts. Originally written in Chinese, this work focuses on philosophy as well as on practical application of techniques. As the translator of this book, Thomas Cleary, maintains:

> Systematic questioning and transcending of the boundary between subject and object, acknowledged to have resulted in such breakthroughs (in quantum theory and the physiology of perception) in Western science, is in fact one of the bases of traditional Chinese science, which has also made breakthroughs in energy and perception . . . This book . . . calls upon both traditional and modern concepts to explain the extraordinary developments of mind and body produced by the science of higher Chinese martial arts.[28]

A contemporary of Leonard's, W. Timothy Gallwey, made extensive use of somewhat Westernized modes of Eastern thought in his two books, *The Inner Game of Tennis* (1974) and *Inner Tennis: Playing the Game* (1976). Among the popular misconceptions that Gallwey attempts to dispose of is the one that equates Eastern ways of competition with not wanting to win. As Gallwey explains:

> Some people have assumed that the Inner Game means not striving to win, not making an effort, avoiding serious competition, and simply playing for the fun of it. But this is not the goal of the Inner Game. Rather, its purpose is to help those who practice it to overcome obstacles which prevent the fullest expression of one's potential.[29]

It certainly can be said of Gallwey that he rather freely adapts Eastern principles to suit his purposes and that he understands competition in a different vein than Kitaro Nishida. Indeed, Gallwey represents an attempt to integrate meditational techniques into a skills teaching-oriented book and, more importantly, an attempt to alter the focus of competitive sport from being against an opponent to being fully involved in the action.

Another recent (1992) attempt to integrate Eastern ideas with Western ones in the field of Sport is Huang and Lynch's groundbreaking *Thinking Mind, Dancing Body*. This book focuses on instruction for the athlete who would maximize his or her performance by implementing specific thinking and training techniques. Further, Hendricks and Carlson's 1982 book, *The Centered Athlete*, provides additional useful techniques for improving athletic performance, although this book concentrates on non-team sports such as running and tennis. While the focus of this book is on philosophy rather than on techniques, these books represent important contributions to the literature on how to expand our modes of athletic training.

More than one writer has spoken to the destructive professional model of competition that has dominated for over twenty years. Ironically, in some of the commentaries there are loud echoes of Graves' point of view that professional athletics have little to do with sport. In 1976, Tutko and Bruns, for instance, opined that:

> If the professionals continue to be the most important model for childhood sports, it will eventually destroy sports as we know them. The pro influence, rather than serve as a virtuous model, will squeeze out the simple joys and satisfactions of playing a game with friends while substituting the dog-eat-dog ethics of the rest of society.[30]

Although Tutko and Bruns present issues of competition in a rather simplistic way at times, they speak eloquently about the need to de-emphasize winning and losing and to search diligently for alternative paradigms of competition, especially for children.

Another writer in the 1970s, Terry Orlick, made an impassioned plea for less violent models for children who look to professional sport figures. Orlick cites the retirement speech of the professional football player George Sauer, then compares Sauer's words with those of a professional hockey executive:

> 'We shouldn't be out there trying to destroy each other, but some people try to make it that way. They have an idea that in order to be really aggressive and obtain the height of football excellence, you have to despise your opponent. I think when you get around to teaching ideas of hatred just to win a ball game, then you're really alienating people from each other and from themselves and are making them strive for false values'. . . .

Yet listen to Toronto Maple Leaf president Harold Ballard: 'I like a defenseman who will be real tough and nasty. I'm looking for a guy who you can toss red meat to and he will go wild.'[31]

Although Orlick's view of competition may be well out of the American mainstream (he is, in fact, Canadian), his essential point is simple and worth listening to, for in the intervening decade and a half between the publication of his book and the onset of this year's football and hockey seasons, violence in professional sport has increased dramatically. That is, Orlick maintained that competition and violence are not inextricably linked. Rather, the linkage is the product of our social conditioning and our specific athletic training and coaching. If you change the manner of coaching to focus on performance rather than hatred for your opponent, presumably performance will improve.

The most pessimistic voice of recent years, in terms of the future of American sports, team sports particularly, is Allen Guttmann whose 1988 book, *A Whole New Ball Game*, rues the examples modern team sports set for young people. Guttmann sees little substantive change possible for the future, largely due to the increasing institutionalization of all sports: "except for Little League baseball and its analogs," he writes, " sports have been institutionalized within the educational system."[32] Whether the educational system is prepared to teach a new paradigm for less violent competition is certainly an open question, as Guttman insists. Another book that emphasizes the negative aspects of competition in professional sports is Arnold Beisser's *The Madness in Sports*.

Very recently, Michael Messner and Donald Sabo, both former athletes, have offered a book that strongly attacks the dominant masculine paradigm in sports, *Sex, Power, & Violence in Sports: Rethinking Masculinity*. These authors offer an essentially feminist perspective on the problems of violence in sports, taking on football as a particularly negative model for how men relate to their bodies and to others. As these writers insist about their own experience in organized sport:

> The fact that we both experienced more agony than ecstasy in doing what we loved most, playing sports, made us feel as though something was seriously deficient or wrong with us as individuals. Many years after the ends of our athletic careers, we learned from feminist women to examine our personal experiences and problems within the context of larger social realities. The idea that 'the personal is political' allowed us to see our own bad experiences in sports not as a manifestation of personal failure, but as normal consequences in a system that values

victory over all else, including relationships with others and even one's own health.[33]

Two recent books that deal directly with Eastern philosophic concepts in terms of American sport are Drew Hyland's *Philosophy of Sport* (1990) and Spencer Wertz's *Talking a Good Game* (1991). Hyland connects Abraham Maslow's psychological term "peak experiences" with the type of concentration normally associated with meditational psychological states in an effort to demonstrate that the concentrated effort of Eastern modes of competition have analogs in the experience of Western athletes. Hyland attributes some of the difficulty that Westerners have with Eastern competitive sport philosophy with the vocabulary of Zen.[34]

Wertz makes a full-blown attempt to integrate Zen thinking into a philosophy of sport that should include professionals. It is the pursuit of goals, movement "in the direction of self-improvement and regeneration,"[35] that, according to Wertz, is the essence of the meaning of sport. In this pursuit of goals, he assumes that "perfection" is an aim. However, since he starts from a faulty assumption—that "Oriental philosophy . . . is a logic of cognitive states, a mapping out of the region of consciousness,"[36] he separates the cognitive mind from the experience by positing a goal as the objective of sport. Nevertheless, as another step in the search for less violent, more effectively competitive models, Wertz makes a significant contribution.

One book of essays, *Mind and Body: East Meets West*, merits particular note, for the essays in this volume address a wide range of issues having to do with creating a new paradigm for controlling violence in sport. Of particular value is an essay by Saul Ross on Cartesian Dualism, Tetsunori Koizumi's intriguing "The Importance of Being Stationary: Zen, Relativity, and the Aesthetics of No-Action," Ann Brunner's "Beyond East and West: From Influence to Confluence," and Thomas Hanna's insightful concluding essay, "Physical Education as Somatic Education: A Scenario for the Future." As Hanna insists, in the past generation, large segments of our culture have come to "the recognition that one's bodily states and one's mental states are inseparably connected. Without anyone realizing it, the past twenty years have witnessed the solution of the mind-body problem, not by philosophical debate but by cultural transformation."[37]

Two books that further explore the mind/body/spirit relationship focus on the field of holography: *The Holographic Paradigm and Other Paradoxes*, edited by Ken Wilber, and Michael Talbot's *The Holographic*

Universe. These writers explore the unity of creation from the points of view of physics, quantum mechanics, and philosophy. The power of the mind to affect performance in sport is touched upon by Talbot in reference to an Australian psychologist's experiment.

> He took three groups of basketball players and tested their ability to make free throws. Then he instructed the first group to spend twenty minutes a day practicing free throws. He told the second group not to practice, and had the third group spend twenty minutes a day visualizing that they were shooting perfect baskets. As might be expected, the group that did nothing showed no improvement. The first group improved 24%, but through the power of imagery alone, the third group improved an astonishing 23%.[38]

The role of the mind in creating the reality in which we find ourselves, and the holographic processes by which this reality is created (according to the holographic theory's proponents), offer potential areas for further exploration of how violence in sport can be minimized through training the mind in what Talbot refers to as "resonance." Also, while the field of holographic theory is still in its very early stages, eventually it may provide a bridge for Westerners to better understand the basis of Eastern ways of training for sport.

If the cultural transformation to a new, less violent paradigm in professional sports has already begun or, as Hanna insists, has already happened while no one was watching, there should be some evidence of this change. While I would not go so far as Hanna in claiming that the change has already taken place, certainly books like Pat Riley's *The Winner Within* indicate that portions of a new, less violent, paradigm are now an integral part of at least this coach's mentality. As Riley says about winning basketball: "eventually, every team has to learn that excellence isn't a destination. It's a process that must be continually improved, just as the Japanese view quality to be."[39] Certainly, this is a considerable coaching distance from Vince Lombardi's 1960s statement "I will demand a commitment to excellence and to victory, and that is what life is all about," or George Allen's 1970s dictum, "The winner is the only individual who is truly alive."[40]

The literature about violence in sport is varied and rich. However, there are no extant studies that I have come upon in my research that have attempted to explicate the historical reasons for this violence and to elucidate ways of escaping the worst of the violence, particularly that part of it that is clearly beyond the rules.

Notes

1. Desmond Lee, trans., *The Republic* of Plato (New York: Penguin, 1974), p. 165.
2. Plato, *The Republic*, Desmond Lee, trans. (New York: Penguin, 1974), p. 176.
3. Mark Twain, *A Connecticut Yankee in King Arthur's Court* (New York: Signet, 1963), p. 289.
4. Spencer K. Wertz, *Talking a Good Game: Inquiries into the Principles of Sport* (Dallas: Southern Methodist University Press, 1991), p. 34. As I was unable to procure a copy of Graves' 1900 article, "The Philosophy of Sport," I am here relying largely on Wertz's analysis of Graves.
5. Graves, in Wertz, pp. 36-37.
6. Kenneth Schmitz, "Sport and Play: Suspension of the Ordinary," in William J. Morgan and Klaus V. Meier, eds., *Philosophic Inquiry in Sport* (Champaign, IL: Human Kinetics Publishers, 1988), pp. 31-32.
7. Warren P. Fraleigh, "Why the Good Foul Is Not Good," in William Morgan and Klaus V. Meier, eds., *Philosophic Inquiry in Sport* (Champaign, IL: Human Kinetics Publishers, 1988), p. 269.
8. John C. Phillips and Walter E. Schafer, "Consequences of Participation in Interscholastic Sports: A Review and Perspectus," in *Sport and American Society*, 3rd edition., George H. Sage, ed. (Reading, MA: Addison-Wesley, 1970), p. 188.
9. George Sage, "Humanism in Sport," in *Sport and American Society*, 3rd ed. (Reading, MA: Addison-Wesley, 1980), p. 365.
10. David Riesman and Reuel Denney, "Football in America: A Study in Cultural Diffusion," in John Loy and Gerald Kenyon, eds. *Sport, Culture, and Society* (New York: Macmillan, 1969), p. 318.
11. Robert G. Osterhoudt, ed., *The Philosophy of Sport: A Collection of Original Essays* (Springfield, IL: Charles C. Thomas Publisher, 1973), pp. 149-150.
12. Drew Hyland, "Competition and Friendship." *Journal of the Philosophy of Sport*, vol. v, 1978, p. 36.
13. Allan Back and Daeshik Kim, "Towards a Western Philosophy of the Eastern Martial Arts." *Journal of the Philosophy of Sport*, vol. VI, p. 19.
14. Spencer K. Wertz, "Zen, Yoga, and Sports: Eastern Philosophy for Western Athletes." *Journal of the Philosophy of Sport*, IV, 1977. This article, in an updated version, appears in Wertz's book *Talking a Good Game: Inquiries into the Principles of Sport*.
15. Shinobu Abe, "Modern Sports and the Eastern Tradition," p. 46.
16. Shinobu Abe, "Modern Sports and the Eastern Tradition of Physical Culture: Emphasizing Nishida's Theory of the Body." *Journal of the Philosophy of Sport*, vol. XIV, 1987, p. 44.

17. Peter King, "Halt the Head-hunting." *Sports Illustrated*, December 19, 1994, p. 27.
18. Mike Preston, "The Breaks of the Game." *The Baltimore Sun*, December 28, 1994, p. 1C.
19. Paul Weiss, *Sport: A Philosophic Inquiry* (Carbondale, IL: Southern Illinois University Press, 1969), p. 243.
20. Wertz, p. 23.
21. Earle F. Ziegler, *Sport and Physical Education Philosophy* (Dubuque, Iowa: Benchmark Press, 1989), p. 336. See also *Physical Education and Sport Philosophy* (Englewood Cliffs, NJ: Prentice-Hall, 1977) and *Problems in the History and Philosophy of Physical Education and Sport* (Englewood Cliffs, NJ: Prentice-Hall, 1968).
22. Ziegler, *Sport and Physical Education Philosophy*, p. 337.
23. Harold J. Vanderzwaag, *Toward a Philosophy of Sport* (Reading, MA: Addison-Wesley, 1972).
24. Glenn Dickey, *The Jock Empire: Its Rise and Fall* (Radnor, PA: Chilton Book Company, 1974).
25. Don Atyeo, *Blood & Guts, Violence in Sports* (New York: Paddington Press, 1979), p. 371.
26. John Underwood, *Spoiled Sport: A Fan's Notes on the Troubles of Spectator Sports* (New York: Little, Brown, and Company, 1984), p. 96.
27. George Leonard, The Ultimate Athlete: Re-Visioning Sports, Physical Education, and the Body (New York: Viking, 1974), pp. 48-49.
28. Shi Ming and Siao Weijia, *Mind over Matter: Higher Martial Arts* (Berkeley, CA: Frog, Ltd. Books, 1994), p. vii.
29. W. Timothy Gallwey, *Inner Tennis: Playing the Game* (New York: Random House, 1976), pp. 137-138. Also see *The Inner Game of Tennis* (New York: Random House, 1974).
30. Thomas Tutko and William Bruns, Winning Is Everything and Other American Myths (New York: Macmillan, 1976), p. 51.
31. Terry Orlick, *Winning Through Cooperation* (Washington, D.C.: Acropolis Books, 1978), p. 104.
32. Allen Guttmann, *A Whole New Ball Game: An Interpretation of American Sports* (Chapel Hill, NC: University of North Carolina Press, 1988), p. 189.
33. Michael A. Messner and Donald F. Sabo, *Sex, Violence & Power in Sports: Rethinking Masculinity* (Freedom, CA: The Crossing Press, 1994), p. 10.
34. Drew Hyland, *Philosophy of Sport* (New York: Paragon House, 1990), pp, 77-84.
35. Wertz, p. 45.
36. Wertz, p, 111.
37. Thomas Hanna, "Physical Education as Somatic Education: A Scenario of the Future," in *Mind and Body: East Meets West*, Seymour Kleinman, ed. (Champaign, IL: Human Kinetics Press, 1984), p. 177.

38. Michael Talbot, *The Holographic Universe* (New York: HarperCollins, 1991), p. 88.
39. Pat Riley, *The Winner Within: A Life Plan for Team Players* (New York: G.P. Putnam's Sons, 1993), p. 151.
40. Quoted in James A. Michener, *Sports in America* (New York: Random House, 1976), pp. 420-421.

Chapter 3

℘〰℺

Violence in Western Sports

Violence and sports have been intimately linked since the earliest recorded history of Western culture, and professional sports have always served to increase the level of violence over that experienced in purely amateur sports. Indeed, just as it is today, money and prizes tend to change the focus of sport from the game itself to the rewards for playing the game. Following is a brief history of how sports and violence have come to be intertwined in Western culture, for without an understanding of where we have been, we cannot fully appreciate either how we have evolved culturally or the need to continue our evolutionary process.

The Homeric Tradition

The earliest mention of sports in the Western literary tradition is in the Homeric epic poem *the Iliad*, probably written in the eighth century B.C.[1] However, the poem was written about events that quite likely occurred several centuries earlier, perhaps as early as the twelfth century B.C. and it is impossible to discern whether Homer was writing about the sports practices during his own time or whether he had access to historical material about the athletic events held during the Trojan War, material that has since disappeared from existence.

At any rate, even in *the Iliad*, recognizable prizes are offered to the victors in the games that are held at the funeral of Achilles' friend, Patroclos, prizes that would certainly constitute professional rewards, even in the modern world. The chariot race, for instance, had prizes even for fifth place, and the connection between winning, alcohol, and sexual rewards was already obvious:

> First for charioteers he set the prizes: a girl adept at gentle handicraft to be taken by the winner, and a tripod holding twenty-six quarts, with handle-rings. For the runner-up he offered a six-year-old unbroken mare, big with a mule foal. For third prize a fine cauldron of four gallons, never scorched, bright as on casting day, and for the fourth two measured bars of gold; for fifth, a new two-handled bowl.[2]

The tripod and the cauldron would have held wine, and gold was then not so precious a commodity as it has become in today's money-fixated world; hence, it is given to the fourth place finisher. Nevertheless, the prizes were sufficient to create a heated battle among the charioteers on the plains of Troy. Moreover, the spectators—both the Greek gods watching from Olympus and the men watching at the finish line—became involved in the sport, sometimes in ways not unknown today.

The Greek gods were certainly a partisan lot of spectators, throwing their immortal weight behind their favorites in ways designed to tip the balance, like gamblers intent on fixing a game. When Athena sees that Apollo has "struck the flashing whip" out of her favorite's, Diomedes', hands, she gives Diomedes his whip back, and goes after Apollo's choice, Eumelos, "and cracked his yoke in two."[3]

Moreover, the spectators behave rather like soccer of football spectators of today, partisan and insulting to their opponents' fans. When Idomeneus, one of Diomedes' countrymen, says he sees his friend in the lead, Aias takes him to task: "Not by a long shot are you.../the one who has the best eyes in his head./But you always have something to say." This prompts an angry retort: "No one [is] like you/for picking fights and giving foolish counsel; otherwise you rank last among the Argives,/ having a mind like a hoof."[4]

The participants, too, engage in a kind of trash talk, complaining about their fellow competitors' recklessness, as is the case when Menelaos yells at Antilokhos, "no man in the world is a more dangerous pest than you are."5 Even after the race, the second place finisher complains that the result was unfair, that the winner cheated. Although they barely avoid coming to blows, due to the intercession of Achilleus, the sense of being at the edge of violence dominates the chariot race, from the gods, to the fans, to the participants, not unlike the atmosphere created at a modern professional football game.

The Greek Olympics

The games at the funeral of Patroclos were seen only by the gods and the Greek troops massed on the plains of Troy, but by shortly after 776 B.C., "the traditional date of the first Olympic Games,"6 large crowds were the rule, rather than the exception. Indeed, great religious and cultural festivals in various cities in Greece drew people from relatively far away, some as religious pilgrims, but others as spectators for the entertainments that came to dominate the festivals. H.A. Harris, in his book *Sport in Greece and Rome*, offers the following explanation of why these events came to have so much importance in Greek culture:

> There were two reasons for the connection of athletics with these religious festivals. The Greeks were strongly anthropomorphic in their conception of their deities, and assumed that what gave pleasure to themselves—music, drama, or sport—would equally be gratifying to the gods. Even stronger was the consideration that the large crowds which assembled for the festivals provided spectators for the Games . . . Athletic sports and chariot races were important at all these centers, but at Olympia they were supreme. The assembling of athletes from so many widely separated cities clearly imposed the necessity of some standardization in the rules of the events of the Games.7

Unfortunately, relatively little evidence has survived from the earliest Olympic games, before the "Golden Age" of Greece in the fourth century B.C. However, a few of the stadia survive as ruins, and some literary references about the games are still extant in early Greek writings. Moreover, some aspects of sports contests can be inferred from such things as paintings on pottery and from statuary. For instance, while the athletes in later Olympic games were nude, in the seventh century B.C., it is evident from pottery that the participants wore shorts.

The prizes distributed at the Greek athletic contests during the early centuries of the Olympics were generally sufficient to encourage a class of professional athletes, for they were of substantial value, as Harris notes in *Greek Athletes and Athletics*: "An inscription of the fourth century B.C. tells us that prizes for boys' and youths' events in Athens varied between thirty and sixty amphorae of oil, awards well worth having."[8] Harris goes on to puncture the myth that Greek athletes were simply competing as "paragons of the purest amateurism in sport.:

> The facts hardly support this roseate view. The winner of an event in one of the great . . . festivals was on to a very good thing. He expected to be substantially and materially rewarded by his city for the glory which his victory had brought it. If Plutarch is to be believed, Solon, when legislating for Athens around 590 B.C., laid down maxima for these grants, 500 drachmae for an Olympic victor, 100 for an Isthmian [a biennial athletic festival]. Even the smaller Isthmian award was almost as much as a year's earnings of a working man.[9]

While most of the Olympic competitors came from the wealthier classes (for, as is still true today, most working class citizens had no time or money to train and travel), "even at this early period . . . athletes were not drawn exclusively from a narrow social class . . . It may be that wealthy patrons sometimes helped promising athletes from the working class who could not otherwise have afforded to compete."[10] In fact, quasi-professional sports, in the model of the old East European Communist nations such as East Germany and the Soviet Union, were not unknown in ancient Greece. As Harris notes, states often paid the way of individual athletes, and sometimes subsidized teams raised and entered by the state.[11]

Nor were the games these athletes played without violence; indeed, the level of violence was often far greater than anything seen in modern times. For instance, the original wrestling matches, at least as it has come down to us through the legends of antiquity, were often to the death. In this regard, a Greek vase from around 900 B.C. depicts "a pair of wrestlers attempting to gouge each other's eyes with their thumbs while the onlooker, presumably a referee, stands poised with a pronged stick ready to intervene."[12]

Of course, the Greeks also included the sport of boxing in their athletic festivals, and, as in today's Thai boxing, it is evident that kicking was allowed. Moreover, though the boxers wore leather thongs to protect their hands, there were no breaks in the bouts, and they resembled bar-room brawls in terms of their adherence to any commonly accepted rules.

Indeed, Lucilius and other satiric writers of the time, as is still true today, had a field day with commenting on boxing and boxers. In one epigram, for instance, Lucilius warns an old, worse-for-the-wear fighter "never to look at his own reflection in a pool, or he will die like Narcissus, but for very different reasons."[13] That is, instead of being overwhelmed by his beauty, the washed up fighter will die from the reflection of his fighting-produced ugliness.

But the violence in Olympic boxing and wrestling was exaggerated in a uniquely Greek event, called the *pankration*.[14] As Don Atyeo comments, the *pankration* "wedded, and . . . intensified, the violence" of wrestling and boxing. Further, it had aspects that are much like modern day judo:

> Unlike wrestling where contestants strove to win by unbalancing each other, combatants in the *pankration* tried either to force a submission . . . , immobilize an opponent by breaking his limbs, or kill him, usually with a strangle hold. Although certain tactics such as biting and gouging were specifically banned, the *pankration* was essentially a brutal free-for-all.[15]

Harris, while acknowledging that gouging and biting were technically disallowed in this most brutal contest, admits that often the rules were blatantly broken. Indeed, in a humorous comparison to present-day athletes, Harris describes ancient Greek sport behavior in a way that might still pertain to a Dallas Cowboy-San Francisco 49ers football game: "It is notorious that no player of any game ever starts dirty play. When guilty of the most blatant foul he always claims that he acts in retaliation. So no Greek pankratist ever gouged; he only 'gouged back' or gave 'dig for dig . . .'."[16]

Ancient Rome and Sports Violence

Much of the culture of ancient Rome, including many of its athletic events, is of Greek origin. Nevertheless, the function of athletics in the two cultures was vastly different, for the festivals from which such Greek games as the Olympics emerged "had links with religious observance,"[17] while in Rome the entire purpose of sports events focused on entertainment. As Harris explains, in Rome, "athletics meetings were introduced by ambitious politicians as an amusement to gratify the people . . . Such appeal as they had was chiefly to the leisured and literate classes."[18]

Thus, in Rome, a class distinction between athletes and spectators was evident. Whereas in Greece, the ruling class participated in athletics, perhaps as a residual manifestation of tribal leadership, in Rome the professional athletes who performed in the Circus were looked down upon by the literate classes, as Seneca makes clear in *Epistulae Morales*:

> It is foolish and quite unfitting for an educated man to spend all his time on acquiring bulging muscles, a thick neck, and mighty lungs. . . . Those who dedicate themselves to this way of life have many drawbacks to suffer. There are hours of training which exhaust them and render them unable to concentrate on any worthwhile studies. The large amounts they are compelled to eat make them dull-witted. They have to submit to trainers of the lowest class, men whose minds cannot rise above the boxing ring and the bar, whose highest ambition is to get up a good sweat and then starve to make room for enough drink to put the moisture back.[19]

The class distinction between athletes and spectators may help account for the increasing level of violence in Roman athletic events, for the participants risked life and limb in a way that the Roman upper classes left to the less fortunate.

Perhaps boxing, with its obviously violent intentions, best illustrates how Rome adapted Greek sports to its more violent purposes. Whereas in ancient Greece, pugilists wore soft thongs, principally to protect their hands from injury, by the time of Imperial Rome, these soft gloves had metamorphosed into the *caestus*, a lead-filled leather glove, sometimes studded with metal spikes. As Atyeo notes, with the spiked gloves, "the fighter landing the first solid blow was usually the winner."[20]

Roman sporting events could be quite bloody, indeed, the gladiatorial events certainly representing the pinnacle of such violent entertainment. Like the Greek Olympics, the gladiatorial games had their roots in religious ceremony, principally in funeral rites, but unlike with the Greeks, the religious aspects of the games were dropped in favor of spectacle. As Atyeo explains:

> Gladiatorial combat originated as an Etruscan funeral rite sometime around the sixth century BC. The Etruscans believed that the spirits of the deceased were propitiated by human blood and so it was their

custom to have small numbers of slaves fight to the death before a corpse. This ritual was inherited by the Romans who, in keeping with their pronounced taste for blood and battle, soon dispensed with the religious aspects and savored the spectacle purely as sport.[21]

No violence in modern team sport, not even the soccer riots in Europe or the post-Super Bowl riots in the winning team's city, comes close to the chaos of the worst of the gladiatorial games, the ones thrown by the Roman Emperor, Titus, at the inauguration of the Colosseum in 80 A.D. In addition to many to-the-death duels between pairs of men conscripted into gladiatorial service, there were "spectacular massacres pitting mounted warriors clad in chain mail . . . against charioteers," as well as armies which "set upon each other in a lethal game of human chess in which the pieces were replaced the instant they fell."[22] Thus, whatever connections can be drawn between American football and gladiatorial games (and many such connections can be drawn), the level of violence in the gladiatorial games was far more lethal.

Of course, since many of those who died in the entertainment combats of Imperial Rome were slaves, were prisoners of war, or were from the lowest social classes, the bloodshed hardly mattered to the citizens who comprised the audience for the games. Indeed, Roman slaves were not considered to be humans and had no rights within the society, not even the right to their own life. Yet, connections to our culture's fortunately more genteel standards can be, and have been, made. As Atyeo states, "for many Romans, the fact that gladiators died in the arena was as incidental as the split faces and broken noses are to modern fans. . . ."[23]

In Rome, violence was a culturally accepted phenomenon, both because of its caste system that created an underclass of slaves and the very poor and because it was a war-like society that clearly connected sport and battle, the religious underpinnings of sport that predominated in ancient Greece having receded in the wake of violent mass entertainments.

Little has been written about sports in the cultural development of Europe in the long stretch of history between the fall of the Roman Empire and the onset of the Industrial Revolution in the 19th century. It can be assumed that certain sports continued in some form from Europe's Roman and Greek heritage—boxing and wrestling, for instance, probably maintained a degree of popularity, and prizes were undoubtedly given to the winners of some of these contests. Generally, however, whatever development of games occurred during this time is hidden from our historical view.

It could be maintained that the competitive impulse that leads people to participate in games emerged in a distorted way in such events as burnings at the stake or duels for honor. Certainly (to make a pun), the stakes were quite high at such events. However, it is beyond the scope of this book to speculate on the psychological underpinnings of such displaced competitive venues.

Violence and American Sports

While it is certainly true that Imperial Rome was a most violent society, war and slavery among its basic assumptions, the history of sports violence in more recent times is also frighteningly rich.

Before approximately 1850, America was essentially a rural society, and sports were not a focus of leisure activity, although many Native Americans did participate in sometimes quite brutal team sports such as the original version of lacrosse. What sports there were in the Colonial era, for instance, were not normally team sports but were largely limited to horse racing and hunting. Only with the country's urbanization and industrialization in the mid-nineteenth century did team sports of any kind become a significant factor in our culture. As John Rickards Betts indicates, " organization, journalistic exploitation, commercialization, intercommunity competition . . . increased rapidly after 1850 . . . as the Industrial Revolution [altered] the interests, habits, and pursuits of all classes of society."[24]

Lacrosse, however, presents an instance of a team sport that bridged the cultural gap between Native Americans and the white settlers and, in some ways, is a precursor to other, more contemporary, ball sports, including baseball. Like the ancient Greek games, one of the reasons for playing *baggataway* (renamed lacrosse by the early French settlers in Quebec) was in the context of religious ritual, and like the Roman games, one of the reasons for playing was preparation for war.

As might be expected, considerable violence was quite common at these lacrosse matches, particularly when the contest pitted one tribe against another. As Atyeo comments:

How violently the game was played varied from tribe to tribe. Some tribes played with marked good humor, knowing only too well the dangers of a stick swung in anger. Any injuries they received they immediately shrugged off as simply the fortunes of war. Other tribes, however, found it difficult to keep their war games separate from the real thing. After witnessing a Choctaw match which left five players crippled (two of whom subsequently died), one observer noted that the injuries inflicted on a man were frequently avenged by his relatives.[25]

While professional lacrosse leagues died out in Canada and the United States before World War I, for a time they flourished, eliciting occasional spates of journalistic disgust at the level of violence the game institutionalized, one newspaper featuring a headline after a violent match that shouted, "Boxing Is Considered Brutal but Go as Far as You Like in Lacrosse."[26]

It was baseball, however, that became the first American team sport to grab the country's attention fully. By the 1850s, baseball clubs had been organized in the East and Midwest and, although the Civil War halted the spread of baseball during the early 1860s, after 1865, baseball's advance as the "national pastime" had begun in earnest.

In the 1870s, with the development of more and better roads between cities, and the advent of transcontinental railways, professional sports in America were made much more viable. Also, the railways began the commercialization of team sports, the Michigan Central Railroad boasting, in the 1886 edition of *Spalding's Official Base Ball Guide*, that "the cities that have representative clubs contesting for the championship pennant . . . are joined together by the Michigan Central Railroad . . . [which] has enjoyed almost a monopoly of Base Ball travel in former years."[27]

And from the beginning, baseball embraced the culture's tendencies toward violence, as is exemplified in its attitude toward, and in its treatment of, umpires. As previously noted, Mark Twain's somewhat exaggerated claim was that "the umpire's first decision was usually his last; they broke him in two with a bat, and his friends toted him home on a shutter."[28] Even giving Twain's satire a wide berth, the on-the-field violence in the early decades of baseball included umpires, for in America's nineteenth century, the niceties of civilization did not always extend to sport.

Nor was Twain the only commentator on the lot of the umpire in the early decades of baseball. In the famous 1888 humorous parody poem, "Casey at the Bat," the line, "Kill him! Kill the umpire! shouted someone in the stands," spoke to the dangerous lot of umpires. The history of baseball is filled with stories of crowds threatening and beating umpires. One umpire from the early days, Steamboat Johnson, estimated that "he had been the target of some four thousand bottles, twenty of which had found their mark."[29] Moreover, violence in baseball was hardly limited to umpires, even in the early days, for brawls, beanballs, and high spikes were (and often still are) accepted parts of the game.

In terms of acceptability of violence, perhaps hockey traditionally has been the most violent of the professional sports commonly played in America. Indeed, more than twenty years ago, Vaz observed about the training for professional hockey players that the:

> . . . implicit objective is to put the opposing star player out of action without doing him serious harm. Illegal tactics and 'tricks' of the game are both encouraged and taught; rough play and physically aggressive performance are strongly encouraged and sometimes players are taught the techniques of fighting. Minimal consideration is given to the formal normative rules of the game, and the conceptions of sportsmanship and fair play are forgotten. . . . Gradually the team is molded into a tough fighting unit prepared for violence whose primary objective is to win hockey games.[30]

Such training as this is undoubtedly still common among the higher levels of amateur hockey and, despite some moves away from showcasing overt violence, the NHL certainly still provides its share of punches, brawls, and beyond the rules mayhem.

The Dissenters: Violence is Lessening in Sports

Not every commentator agrees that violence in team sports is a growing problem. Eric Dunning, for instance, "has marshaled considerable evidence to prove that legitimate sports violence (i.e., that committed within the rules of the game) has declined over the past several hundred years."[31] Certainly, as Dunning maintains, we no longer tolerate the excesses of Roman gladiatorial combats or the uncontrolled violence of the early football teams.

Another voice claiming that American sports really are not so violent as they might be is provided by Fawcett and Thomas in their book, *America and the Americans*. Among other things, these writers point out that violence among spectators in American professional sports is much rarer than it is in soccer or rugby, for instance.

What violence there is in American sports tends to take place in the game itself, not among the spectators, and this violence is, in turn, diminishing. . . . Compared to sports in other countries, where fighting, bottle throwing, and rioting have long been common, American spectators, certainly at professional games, are curiously passive.[32]

One last view worth noting is that of Oliver Leaman who, in his article "Cheating and Fair Play in Sport," maintains that such violence as exists in professional hockey is morally excusable because:

> . . . both the players and . . . the spectators will expect a skillful player to be good at cheating, where this involves breaking the rules when it is most advantageous to his side. Where such a policy is generally pursued there is no general deception practiced, and players are on equal terms in so far as the conditions for winning the contest are concerned. It is difficult then to see what is morally wrong with such behaviour. After all, it is presumed that the players and spectators are free agents in their participation and attendance.[33]

Of course, as I maintain in chapter 1 and elsewhere, there are moral issues connected to violence in sports that go beyond the voluntary nature of spectator and player, including issues of how we wish children to perceive competition and how we wish sports to adhere to laws the rest of American citizens must obey.

In the following section, I explore what I consider to be the dominant factor in the genesis of our culture's attitudes toward violence in professional sports, a factor which has only been glanced at by most western philosophers of sport and which deserves a great deal more attention: the effect that Western philosophy's split of the concepts of "mind" and "body" has had on how we interact with one another in such events as professional sports.

Mind/Body Dualism: From Plato through Freud

Is it, then, that the same instincts toward violence that allowed the Romans to play lethal games for the entertainment of its citizens has permitted professional hockey fans to cheer the splitting of an opponent's face with a high stick or that murmurs approvingly when the opposition's quarterback is carried off the field on a stretcher? Or is it that the underlying metaphysics of the ethical values that our culture so unquestioningly carries are at least as vital a factor in our violent responses as is instinct?

In the following sections, I first uncover the roots of philosophy's mind/body/spirit split in Plato and Aristotle, ancient Greece's two most prolific and influential thinkers. I trace the continuation of the mind/body/spirit split through the thinking of the 5th century A.D. Christian theologian, Saint Augustine and the 17th century philosopher, Rene Descartes. Next, I pick up the thread of our cultural attitude toward the disunity of mind, body, and spirit with the 19th century thinking of Sigmund Freud, heavily influenced, as it was, by the German pessimistic philosopher, Arthur Schopenhauer. Finally, upon reaching the 20th century, I discuss several alternative views of the philosophy of sports. In Chapter 5, I discuss several writers, principally those who are from Eastern cultures or who borrow heavily from Eastern philosophies, in more detail. These writers' sport philosophies elucidate ways to reunite body, mind, and spirit.

It would be easy to maintain that such violent sports as the *pankration* represent the primitive tendencies of a culture that was only a few centuries removed from the dawn of written history. But such an assertion would ignore important facts, including that violence in our twentieth century culture can easily match that of the ancient Greeks, both in sport and in society in general. Moreover, certain tendencies in Greek culture and philosophy, tendencies which still form the backbone of modern Western culture, contributed to condoning, even encouraging violence as a legitimate mode of action in sport.

One of the tendencies that has contributed to the Western proclivities toward violence in sport stems from the division of the human into two distinct parts: body and soul. This philosophic dualism, so much a part of the Platonic-Christian-Cartesian marrow of our culture, is rarely noticed by Western sport commentators, but it is not a universally accepted notion, and it has a profound effect on how we view the sport world.

Plato was the first of the Greek philosophers to expound on the distinctions between the body and the soul. In *Phaedo*, Plato relates the following dialogue between Socrates and Simmias, a one-sided dialogue that gets to the essence of Western culture's dualistic roots, for it underscores the traditional cultural subordination of body to soul, of form to reason.

[Socrates] . . . Is the very truth of things contemplated by the body? Is it not rather the case that the man who prepares himself most carefully to apprehend by his intellect the essence of each thing which he examines will come nearest to the knowledge of it?

[Simmias] Certainly.

[Socrates] . . . Have we not also said that, when the soul employs the body in any inquiry, and makes use of sight, or hearing, or any other sense . . . she is dragged away by it to the things which never remain the same, and wanders about blindly, and becomes confused and dizzy, like a drunken man dealing with things that are ever-changing?

[Simmias] Certainly.

[Socrates] . . . Consider the matter in yet another way. When the soul and the body are united, nature ordains the one to be a slave and to be ruled, and the other to be master and to rule.[34]

For Plato, the body and the soul were quite separate entities, and it was the soul that merited the attention of the philosopher. That is, Plato "forwards a position that radically separates the body and the spirit" and he had "a negative perception of corporeality."[35] Or, as George Leonard asserts, "in the thought of Plato and others, the entire physical realm has come to be considered a mere shadow of the realm of ideal forms. Ever since the Greeks, if fact, the great majority of our religious leaders and philosophers either have ignored or denigrated the body."[36] In *Phaedo*, the body is seen as actually impeding the spirit's progress. "The philosopher releases his soul from communion with the body, so far as he can . . . [for] intercourse with the body troubles the soul, and hinders her from gaining truth and wisdom."[37]

Furthermore, sports were considered to be essentially a sub-category of military preparations, not an end in themselves. Of course, to a large degree, this emphasis on the military probably reflects the harsh necessities of life in Athens, and Athens' main political opponent, Sparta, certainly emphasized sports as an integral part of their highly militaristic society. The main connection between mind and body, as far as sports were concerned, had to do with the need of the body to be tempered by the more spiritual nature of the mind.

. . . there is the man who takes a lot of strenuous physical exercise and lives well, but has little acquaintance with literature or philosophy. The physical health that results from such a course first fills him with confidence and energy, and increases his courage. . . . But what happens if he devotes himself exclusively to it, and has no intelligent interests? Any latent love he may have for learning is weakened by being starved of instruction or inquiry and by never taking part in any discussion or educated activity, and becomes deaf and blind because its perceptions are never cleared and it is never roused or fed.[38]

When Augustine, one of the foremost theological fathers of the early Christian church, looked for a way to view the mind/body/spirit connection, he found a sympathetic philosophy in Plato. That is, like Plato, Augustine nurtured a profound mistrust for the cravings of the body, and a specific distaste for the sexual impulse as a manifestation of original sin, for Augustine believed that death came into the world as a direct punishment of Adam and Eve's sin. That sin separated the body from the spirit and, since then, Christianized Western philosophers have generally toed the line that Augustine drew between the wisdom of the spirit and the coarseness and sinfulness of the body. Indeed, as Irving Singer noted: "Augustine . . . defined his life as a constant struggle between the two poles of his dualistic conception—the citadel of nature and the city of God, the cravings of the body and the yearnings of the soul, the one that is based on desire and the one that seeks renunciation."[39] In the Islamic tradition, too, there has been a tendency to separate the mind and the body, at least as far back as the 12th-century. In Cordoba, at that time under Islamic rule, a famous debate transpired between the Islamic philosopher, Ibn Arabi, and the scholar, Averroes, concerning the relationship of mind and body. Ibn Arabi "argued that the empirical study of the physical world should not be separated from religion; Averroes' arguments carried the day."[40]

Thus, the separation of body, mind, and spirit that began with Plato seeded the thinking of Christian philosophers and theologians a thousand years later, and the mistrust for the body has, ever since, colored our culture's view of sports. Too much emphasis on the body's abilities was suspect, for the mind and spirit were considered to be of a higher order than the body, and this line of thinking appealed to the dominant strain of Christian thinkers, including Rene Descartes (1596-1650), the influential French mathematician and philosopher.

Descartes arrived at his agreement with Platonic and Augustinian notions of the separation of body from mind and spirit partly due to his exceedingly mechanistic view of the world. As Jamake Highwater maintains:

> Descartes inaugurated a major shift to a paradigm with which, to a very great extent, we are still living today. Despite its scientific tone, his dualism and his deprecation of the physical world as 'dead matter' was profoundly Christian. It resonated with Augustinian morality, and therefore made Christian dogma the premise upon which a supposedly nonreligious and objectified science was built . . . In much the way that the Church was focused upon the disembodied soul, Descartes was concerned with rationality as a disembodied process.[41]

The insidious effects of Cartesian dualism remain with us as often unexamined root assumptions among scientific and Christian thinkers, philosophers, and psychologists. When the world is viewed as a "Great Machine," as Descartes held, it is possible to treat the world, human relationships, human activities such as sport, and the human species' place in the world, quite differently than if one treats the mind, body, and spirit as a single, unfragmented whole. Thus, while Descartes is responsible for formulating analytical geometry, "a way of drawing pictures of relationships between different measurements of time and distance [that is] a wonderful tool for organizing a wealth of scattered data into one meaningful pattern . . . The starting point of this process is a mental attitude which initially perceives the physical world as fragmented and different experiences as logically unrelated."[42]

The view that spirit, mind, and body are separate entities can be traced back at least to Plato in our written tradition, and the tendency to separate the body from the spirit was formalized in Western culture in the philosophical/theological writings of the early Church fathers, including Augustine and later thinkers such as Descartes. By the 19th century, as the Industrial Revolution began to alter European and, later, American culture, and as Darwinian scientific rationalism came to be the dominant philosophic strain, the separation of the elements of the human psyche and spirit took a new turn. Sigmund Freud, arguably the most dominant intellectual voice of the late 19th and early 20th century, eliminated the spirit from the mind/body/spirit triad and separated the mind into the now-familiar elements of ego, id, and superego. The body was reduced to an instrument to act out our sexual impulses, whether directly or symbolically.

It is in the bleak philosophy of Arthur Schopenhauer that Freud found his most obvious antecedent. Schopenhauer repeatedly emphasized the illusion of individuality and the absence of any spiritual framework for existence, taking his cue from the language of evolutionary theory and scientific rationalism.

The explicit acceptance of Schopenhauer's version of the dominance of human sexual impulses in determining the direction of the individual psyche certainly places Freud within the spectrum of scientific rationalism that characterized intellectual thought in the first half of the twentieth century. Nevertheless, Freud's theories, however important they may have been in creating the field of psychology, must be viewed as severely limited by the faulty assumptions that permeate them.

The Freudian tradition emphasizes the image of the sexual drive as a biological necessity that attempts to express itself despite the rules devised to control it by culture and civilization. The Freudian view gave impetus to the concept that we are only civilized to the extent that we have been able to suppress our animalistic and sexual instincts. Unfortunately, this archaic notion still has immense authority.[43]

Positivistic ideas so permeate current scientific methods that we have entirely separated mind from body in most mainstream Western science in the past century. As Willis Harman notes, the great debunking of religion by science meant that "only what could be physically measured could be studied by science, and only what was studied by science was real."[44]

Thus, the Platonic and Christian tendency to view the body as a poor step-child to the mind and/or spirit, the Darwinian notion of "survival of the fittest," and the Freudian theory of a sexuality that covertly controls the mind and psyche's responses to human interactions all contributed vital elements to our culture's current view of sport. Competition, according to the cultural amalgam we have made of these theories, is the natural state of affairs, as we strive to be the top of the evolutionary heap. Cooperation fits into this theory, not as the natural state of existence, but as a strategy applicable mostly to team sports.

But the increasing cultural mixing of the 20th century, brought on partly by our greatly expanded communications abilities, has brought us other ways of looking at the mind/body/spirit relationship, ways that emphasize the unity of these three human elements. Although American sports may still be premised on the competitive model fostered by our culture's dualistic religious, psychological, and scientific-rationalist background, ideas from Eastern philosophies have made inroads into how sports are thought of, and written about, in our contemporary culture. These newer ideas, which are in reality older than even Plato's writings, emphasize cooperation and a sense of inner and joint purpose to sports and games. When answered from a perspective that views mind, body, and spirit as separate entities, and views the body as a lesser and degraded partner, the question "what is sport?" implies an answer that insists on sports' unimportance. Of course, many contemporary writers in the emerging field of philosophy of sport reflect, to one degree or another, our cultural roots, in that their very definition of "sport" is premised on the principle that competition reflects man's innate character.

In the following chapter (4), I discuss the various administrative options available for diminishing the level of violence in professional sports. Then, in Chapter 5, I offer a view of competition that rejects the traditional Western mind/body dualism in favor of a more unitary view.

Notes

1. Although sports are also played in Homer's other epic poem *The Odyssey*, there are no scenes of large games; rather they take place as a sort of after-dinner entertainment.
2. Homer, *The Iliad*, Robert Fitzgerald, trans. (Garden City, NY: Doubleday, 1974), pp. 543-544.
3. Ibid., p. 547.
4. Ibid., p. 550.
5. Ibid., p. 549.
6. H.A. Harris, Sport in Greece and Rome (Ithaca, NY: Cornell University Press, 1972), p. 15.
7. Harris, *Sport in Greece and Rome*, p. 16.
8. H.A. Harris, *Greek Athletes and Athletics* (Bloomington, IN: Indiana University Press, 1966), p. 36.
9. Harris, *Greek Athletes and Athletics*, p. 37.
10. Ibid.
11. Ibid.
12. Don Atyeo, *Blood & Guts: Violence in Sports* (New York: Paddington Press, 1979), p. 129.
13. Harris, *Greek Athletes and Athletics*, p. 101.
14. "Pankration" translates as "all strength."
15. Atyeo, p. 130.
16. Harris, *Greek Athletes and Athletics*, p. 107.
17. Harris, *Sport in Greece and Rome*, p. 72.
18. Ibid., p. 73.
19. Seneca, *Epistulae Morales* XV, 2.
20. Atyeo, p. 131.
21. Atyeo, p. 131.
22. Atyeo, p. 133.
23. Atyeo, p. 134.
24. John Rickards Betts, "The Technological Revolution and the Rise of Sport, 1850-1900." *Mississippi Valley Historical Review*, XL (September, 1953), p. 231.
25. Atyeo, p. 202.
26. Atyeo, p. 203.
27. Betts, pp. 233-234.
28. Mark Twain, *A Connecticut Yankee in King Arthur's Court* (New York: Signet, 1963), p. 289.
29. Atyeo, p. 268.
30. E. Vaz, "The culture of young hockey players: initial observations." In A. Taylor, ed., *Training: Scientific Basis and Applications.* Quebec: Laval University, 1972, p. 230.

31. Guttmann, 1988, p. 160.
32. Edmund Fawcett and Tony Thomas, *America and the Americans* (New York: Fontana/Collins, 1982), pp. 394-95.
33. Oliver Leaman, "Cheating and Fair Play in Sport." In *Philosophic Inquiry in Sport*, ed. W.J. Morgan and K.V. Meier, (Champaign, IL: Human Kinetics Publishers, 1988), p. 279.
34. Plato, *Phaedo*, trans. F.J. Church (New York: MacMillan, 1985) in *Philosophic Inquiry in Sport*, ed. W.J. Morgan and K.V. Meier (Champaign, IL: Human Kinetics Publishers, 1988), pp. 82-83.
35. Morgan and Meier, pp. 77-78.
36. George Leonard. *The End of Sex: Erotic Love After the Sexual Revolution* (Los Angeles: J.P. Tarcher, 1983), p. 139.
37. Plato, *Phaedo*, trans. by F.J. Church (New York: MacMillan, 1985).
38. Plato, *The Republic*. Desmond Lee, trans. (New York: Penguin, 1974), pp. 175-176.
39. Irving Singer, *The Nature of Love: Courtly and Romantic*, Volume 2 (Chicago: University of Chicago Press, 1984) p. 131.
40. Willis W. Harman, "The Changing Image of Man/Woman: Signs of a Second Copernican Revolution." In *Mind and Body: East Meets West*, Seymour Kleinman, ed. Champaign, IL: Human Kinetics Press, 1986, p. 3.
41. Jamake Highwater, *Myth and Sexuality* (New York: New American Library, 1990), pp. 154, 156.
42. Gary Zukav, *The Dancing Wu Li Masters: An Overview of the New Physics* (New York: William Morrow, 1979), p. 322.
43. Highwater, *Myth and Sexuality*, pp. 3-4.
44. Harman, p. 4.

Chapter 4

℘ℛ

Current Administrative and Legal Remedies to Violence in American Professional Sport

Introduction

The endemic violence in American team sports demands that certain issues and questions be directly addressed by our society. First, it has been necessary to ask what the history and scope of violence has been in sport. This question was addressed in the previous chapter and in Chapter 1. Second, hypothetically, what should be done about such violence on the playing fields? This question implicitly includes coming to an understanding of what is natural aggression versus controllable violence. Third, practically speaking, what can be done legally and administratively about outside of the rules violence in American professional team sports? Fourth, are there philosophical principles that will allow us, over time, to create a cultural framework for professional sport that will tend to ameliorate the excesses of violence that are too prevalent today in professional team sports?

In the following two sections, I discuss the second and third of the above questions. The fourth question, concerning philosophical principles, is the focus of Chapter 5, although in the following section of this chapter ("Violence as Instinct or Training?"), some of the issues discussed in more detail in Chapter 5 are introduced. The section titled "Changes Aimed at Curbing Violence" is further subdivided into (1) administrative options and (2) legal remedies.

Violence: Instinct or Training?

The question of whether humans are, by nature, violent has been argued by psychologists, biologists, philosophers, and anthropologists, among others, for the better part of a century and a half, particularly since Charles Darwin posited his Theory of Evolution. In the 20th century, Sigmund Freud and others of the first generations of psychologists joined the debate on the instinctual side, Freud's notion that man has a basically untrustworthy inner nature giving evidence for Darwin's competitive "survival of the fittest" theory. Then, in the middle of the 20th century, the voices of anthropologists were added to the argument, many of the loudest ones on the side of considering man an instinctually violent creature.

A distinction must here be made between two words: "violence" and "aggression." In the context of this book, "aggression" means "forceful action," though not necessarily of a physical sort only. Aggression, in this sense, is the power of energy directed into mental or physical action. "Violence" differs from "aggression" in that it is specifically aimed at physically harming others, and it happens in clear contravention of the intent of the rules of the sport.

Such anthropological writers as Konrad Lorenz, Niko Tinbergen, Robert Ardrey, and Desmond Morris maintain that humans are universally and instinctively aggressive. They cite evidence from archeological digs, as well as from recorded human history, that emphasizes mankind's tendency to glorify war and war's violence. Included in this analysis of archeology and history are such "objective" data as Moche pottery from Peru which "depicts triumphant soldiers celebrating over abject prisoners,"[1] and our well-documented 20th century tendency toward genocidal spasms, such as the Holocaust and, more recently, mass murders in Cambodia, Rwanda, and Bosnia. Raymond Dart, in his 1953 essay, "The predatory transition from ape to man," a dark, post-World War II vision of human origins, summed up this view in quite vividly graphic (and enormously subjective) prose:

The blood-bespattered, slaughter-gutted archives of human history from the earliest Egyptian and Sumerian records to the most recent atrocities of the Second World War accord with early universal cannibalism, with animal and human sacrificial practices or their substitutes in formalized religions and with the worldwide scalping, head-hunting, body-mutilating, and necrophiliac practices of mankind in proclaiming this bloodlust differentiator, this predacious habit, this mark of Cain that separates man dietetically from his anthropoidal relatives and allies him rather with the deadliest of Carnivora.[2]

In the field of psychology, Freud certainly believed in a deep, innate aggression in humans: that humans are not gentle, friendly creatures wishing for love and that a powerful measure of desire for aggression has to be reckoned with as part of their instinctual endowment. While "aggression" and "violence" are not identical concepts, in that aggression can include a range of behaviors that stop short of violence, an unchecked aggressive impulse can easily include an overtly violent element.

This pessimism about the aggressive behavior of humans is echoed by Desmond Morris, from an anthropological perspective, who maintains that "altruism will not be a viable proposition in evolutionary terms,"[3] since the human's true nature is necessarily selfish. Cooperation, in Morris' terms, is the exception to the evolutionary rule.

Other popular anthropological writers, such as Loren Eisley, express somewhat more muted views about humankind's aggressive nature; however, they tacitly accede to the view that the human has a basically violent nature. Eisley, in a narrative, highly personal, and distinctly non-academic style, even imaginatively re-creates a sense of competitive aggression between human and wolf in a chapter of his 1969 volume, *The Unexpected Universe.* In this narrative, Eisley has had a brief confrontation with his German shepherd, Wolf, over a fossilized bone the anthropologist has been examining late at night in his study. Drawing from his Darwinian/Freudian disposition to believe the human instinctually violent, their unconscious containing dark, unavoidable elements, Eisley concludes:

And were there no shadows in my own mind, I wondered. Had I not for a moment, in the grip of that savage utterance, been about to respond, to hurl myself upon him over an invisible haunch ten thousand years removed? Even to me the shadows had whispered—to me, the scholar in his study.[4]

However, other academics, including Ashley Montagu, believe in a quite different vision of human aggression. As Montagu, an anthropologist, notes, such authors as Lorenz and Ardrey "write as if all human societies . . . are aggressive. This simply happens to be untrue."[5] Moreover, using the human history of warmaking as evidence that our species is intrinsically and instinctually violent is terribly misleading, as Jacob Bronowski points out: "War, organized war, is not a human instinct. It is a highly planned and cooperative form of theft."[6] This viewpoint is echoed by Montagu: "Most people in civilized societies get involved in wars not because they feel aggressive toward the socially defined 'enemy,' but because their leaders—who themselves are seldom motivated by aggressive feelings—consider it necessary to make war."[7]

If we assume, as many neo-Freudian and Darwinian writers do, that violence is innate and universal, then the only steps that we can take to alleviate excess violence will likely be administrative and legal. Furthermore, even given the best of rules, laws, and their enforcement, if we instinctively gravitate toward violence, a rather high endemic level of violence in certain sports may be inevitable. If the blood lust of the Roman gladiatorial "entertainments" still runs, not merely in our cultural veins, but also in our human genetic code itself, controlling violence in professional sports may be both futile and unnecessary.

Fortunately, there are now a number of intelligent voices making cogent cases that aggression of the overtly violent sort is trained through a long and exceedingly complex process of cultural adaptation. Indeed, the definition of "instinctual" is being challenged as regards the human tendency toward violence. To be sure, not all of these voices would be called "mainstream," at least in the West with its rigid scientific-rationalist academic biases. However, with the rapid breaking down of cultural barriers in what is increasingly a "global village"[8] (with ideas as well as with consumer goods and markets), it is perhaps overdue for the academic mainstream to expand its interpretive vision to include other cultures' ideas, as well as alternative voices within the Western tradition.

Certainly, understanding the nature of aggression in sport, as in other human activities, includes accounting for both the normal aggression that is essential for existence itself in the complex, daily interplay of people and the extraordinary aggression that merits penalties within the world of professional sport—and would often merit prison within the everyday world of ordinary citizens. As one writer, Jane Roberts, maintains, the artificial aggressiveness we often see in our culture, most often (but not exclusively) expressed by males, is the end result of a long process of emotional displacement, not the result of an intrinsic, instinctual tendency toward violence:

> The male's aggressive tendencies, often taken as a basic characteristic of the [human] species itself . . . is an exaggerated, learned aggressive response, not natural in those terms in [humans] . . . or as interpreted in any other species . . . This artificial aggressiveness has nothing to do either, basically, with the struggle for survival. It is the direct result of the fact that the male has been taught to deny the existence within himself of certain basic emotions. . . . His rage turns outward as aggression.[9]

As is discussed in more detail in Chapter 5, the Zen Buddhist way of looking at aggression and violence is premised on the idea that an enormous amount of what in the West we call "instinct," in the East is attributed to training. That is, as in the following Zen teaching story, a disposition to violence is not something that anyone possesses at birth, nor is it inherited from one's parents; rather, it is acquired in the process of cultural and social adaptation.

> A Zen student came to Bankei and complained: 'Master, I have an ungovernable temper. How can I cure it?'
>
> 'You have something very strange,' replied Bankei. 'Let me see what you have.'
>
> 'Just now I cannot show it to you,' replied the other.
>
> 'When can you show it to me?' asked Bankei.
>
> 'It arises unexpectedly,' replied the student.
>
> 'Then,' concluded Bankei, 'it must not be your own true nature. If it were, you could show it to me at any time. When you were born you did not have it, and your parents did not give it to you. Think that over.'[10]

In support of the contention that violent aggression is not inherently part of the human psyche, according to Montagu and others, cooperation can as easily form the basis of a culture as aggression, and there are several cultures that train their members to be non-aggressive. In his landmark 1978 volume, *Learning Non-Aggression*, Montagu describes one culture, the Tasaday of the Philippines, where the training of children is accomplished in a way that makes them distinctively non-aggressive. Citing the work of John Nance, a journalist who spent more than two months living with the Tasaday in the early 1970s, Montagu states that:

> The Tasaday . . . 'are altogether loving people. They have no weapons, and no apparent aggressive impulses' . . . . Nevertheless . . . 'the children showed the egotism one might expect—arguing over a stick, crying for food, slapping at one another' . . . 'classic' aggressive behavior between toddlers . . . The key question, therefore, for Nance was how the Tasaday managed aggression in children so that they grew to be loving adults. The answer would appear to be that from an early age the Tasaday reward cooperative behavior and discourage aggressive conduct, while setting models in themselves for their children to imitate.[11]

The point here is not that professional sports need to control the aggression necessary to compete successfully. Rather, the point is to establish, at least as a legitimate theoretical construct, that violence is not innate within the human psyche: it is at least partly trained into us by our culture.

Nor is it necessary to demonstrate that aggression is truly not part of the human character, for merely living and competing within sports and in other areas of our culture demand a certain level of aggression. However, violence—aggression aimed at doing harm to another—is controllable through a process of education, as Montagu insists:

> The evidence suggests that . . . human beings can learn virtually anything. Among other things, they can learn to be virtually wholly inaggressive. The human genetic constitution is in no way to be regarded as the equivalent of the theological doctrine of predestination. Whatever humanity's potentialities for aggression . . . it is clear that their expression will largely depend upon the environmental stimulation they receive.[12]

Thus, to some extent at least, it should be possible to reprogram the worst excesses of our cultural indoctrination in violence in order to eliminate their manifestations in professional sport. In other words, while strict rules and legal enforcement may be essential to reduce the level of violence in professional sports, a more lasting and profound alteration of cultural consciousness may be possible through a focus on a new paradigm for competitive athletics, one which emphasizes principles of self-control.

By "self-control" here, I do not mean to imply "deprivation," a connection that is commonly made. Rather, "self-control" in this context refers to a pro-active power that the self possesses to consciously affect his or her actions and thoughts. This implies that the individual is not being driven exclusively by instincts. This is analogous to the difference between a person who has not eaten for a week simply because of lack of food and the person who consciously fasts for a week. The person who fasts may experience the lack of food, not as deprivation, but as spiritual, psychological, or political progress, whereas the unwillingly food-deprived person likely will simply experience the lack of food as hunger.

Changes Aimed at Curbing Violence

While changes in the rules to help alleviate the problem of excessive violence are particular to each sport, there are a number of areas that the major American professional team sports share in terms of offering possibilities for change. Some of these changes involve the players, while others principally involve the fans.

Administrative Options

In the Roman gladiatorial games, the fans would, by giving a thumbs up or down signal, determine matters of life and death for competitors. While such institutionalized violence is contrary to the spirit of all contemporary sports, fan violence is a real problem, both in the United States and abroad. Indeed, the February, 1995 killing of a soccer fan in Italy by fans supporting the opposing team made headlines in the United States, and the loutish behavior of English soccer fans in the Netherlands, Italy, and elsewhere in recent years has been widely chronicled in the press around the world.

a. Limit/eliminate the consumption of alcohol

In the United States, fan violence is often tied to the consumption of alcohol, principally beer, and the sale of beer at stadiums presents a thorny problem for many club owners. On the one hand, when things get out of control, the image of their sport suffers, and the consumption of alcohol at games has many times enflamed problems with fan violence. On the other hand, beer represents substantial concessions revenues for the club owners, and drinking beer at games is nearly (begging pardon for the mixed metaphor) "as American as apple pie."

But alcohol often has proven to be the fuel of choice for disruptive fans, as Michener reminds us, citing an infamous 1974 baseball game between the Cleveland Indians and the Texas Rangers. On June 4 of that year, the teams played a game in Cleveland on a ten-cent beer night.

> In the seventh inning, the Texas manager had to close down his bull pen in right field; Cleveland fans were bombarding the relief pitchers with fire crackers and beer cans. But real trouble erupted in the ninth. Photographs taken of the fray show drunken fans invading the field, climbing atop the Texas dugout and threatening the lives of the visiting players. Only quick support from the Cleveland ballplayers averted a tragedy. Said one Texan, 'If it wasn't for the Cleveland players tonight, we would have got killed.'[13]

It is certainly not the case that Americans are the only ones to have problems with drunken fans. In England, there is a long history of alcohol-fueled soccer and rugby riots. In 1980, after the murder of an English soccer fan, for instance, 450 Scottish soccer fans were arrested for "drunkenness, indecent exposure, and assault."[14]

Certainly, fan violence that is exacerbated by alcohol consumption can be controlled reasonably easily, in the sense that beer sales can be controlled. Indeed, a number of tactics have been employed to do this, including stopping all beer sales in the last quarter or the final innings of a game. And using the promise of cheap beer to lure fans to the game must be prohibited, although an increased social consciousness about alcohol and new laws holding the server legally responsible for the drinkers' driving, among other things, have significantly decreased the owners' impetus to serve as much beer as quickly as possible to spectators.

b.   Turn down the noise; get rid of the mascots

George Vecsey, in a recent column for *The New York Times*, led with a headline that pointed to another way that professional sports club owners can help control the level of violence in the stands: "First Off, Calm Down Noise and Mascots." In this column, Vecsey quotes the Houston Rockets basketball player, Vernon Maxwell, who was hit with a ten game suspension after he went into the stands and punched a fan who had been taunting him: "When he began involving my daughter, Amber, in his obscene and racial remarks, I decided I had enough," he explained. In Vecsey's opinion, at least part of the reason that Maxwell felt impelled to strike back was that the crowd at the game had been whipped into a frenzy by a booming loudspeaker system and a team mascot.

> Many teams pay lip service to civil behavior, but are they doing all they can? Teams can cut down on aggression by limiting the use of message boards and loudspeakers. Showing film clips of athletes running into fences or being blasted by hard tackles is dehumanizing. Then there are arenas in Indianapolis and Charlotte where visiting teams are blasted by the whine of racing cars and the shriek of hornets . . . My next step would be to push the button on all mascots. Watching the Phillies Phanatic zooming around the field before a game, bumping into visiting players, making fun of umpires, aggressing people in the stands, is a signal for fans to get rambunctious.[15]

Vecsey does not claim that cutting down on the noise and eliminating the mascots would be more than a "first step," yet these suggestions are eminently sensible, and Vecsey's many years as a close observer of professional sports lend his opinion considerable weight. And, although Vecsey only hints at this in his February 12, 1995, column, it is worth considering what such intentionally raised energy, added to the alcohol imbibed by the spectators, will do once the game is over and the fans spill out onto the streets of their city and back into their private lives. If the home team loses, and no socially sanctioned outlet is available to vent their beer-bolstered frustrations, how many of them will substitute a family member for the opposing team?

c. *Warn and evict overly rowdy fans*

Although Vernon Maxwell has earned his nickname, Mad Max, and his ten game suspension was merited by his inexcusable, criminal actions, rowdy fans are a problem for both the players and less rowdy fans. Not only can they disrupt a game, they can prevent others from enjoying the game, and perhaps returning to another one. Thus, Maxwell's plea that "some reasonable guideline for appropriate fan conduct needs to be adopted," makes good sense, for "it shouldn't be open season on the players."[16]

That is, while heckling is a time-honored tradition at American professional baseball and basketball games, particularly, there must be some line drawn to prevent fans from too actively encouraging retaliation. For instance, do we want to tolerate the racially-based venom that the black hockey goaltender, Grant Fuhr, used to have to endure when he was in the Islanders' net? Or do we want to tolerate fans who spew a continuous tirade of often personal insults at players?

Perhaps the team sports can learn a lesson from how tennis has dealt with one fan, Jim Pierce, the obnoxious, loud-mouthed father of tennis star Mary Pierce. So loutish was Mr. Pierce's behavior during his daughter's matches, he was repeatedly warned he would be evicted. Finally, after a fierce verbal outburst during his daughter's third-round match at the 1992 French Open, tournament officials ejected him from Roland Garros stadium, "pulled his pass and submitted a report to the Women's Tennis Council." Jim Pierce was eventually banned from all tennis events in which his daughter played. Indeed, on November 19, 1992, the WTC passed "the Jim Pierce rule: "an agent, parent or coach can be banned from any or all tour events for his or her courtside conduct—and seven months later the council invoked it against Jim."[17]

d. Institute strong penalties for fighting

When a sporting event degenerates into a brawl, it is almost always too late to effectively administrate, unless there are severe penalties at the administrator's disposal. The most effective penalty, one that is fortunately being used more and more often, particularly in the NHL and NBA, is to eject players from the game, and to suspend them from further games in the case of serious infractions.

John Underwood, in his often insightful 1984 volume, *Spoiled Sport*, relates some Congressional testimony given by a professional hockey player, Jim Korn, about violence in hockey. The House Judiciary Subcommittee on Criminal Justice was considering a "sports violence bill," HR 2263, which "would have provided penalties—a fine of not more than $5,000, imprisonment of not more than a year, or both, for the use of 'excessive physical force' in professional sports events."[18]

After admitting that professional hockey teams all had "enforcers" whose main task was simply "to intimidate opponents," Korn made a remark that, Underwood notes, "should have been burned in the hide of every administrator of sport."

> Korn said he never got into fights at the amateur levels of hockey. He said he never even saw one in the Olympic Games. Why not? Because if you go outside the rules to batter another player in the amateurs, he said, you get ejected—kicked out of the game—and maybe out of future games as well.[19]

In the past several years, hockey has begun enforcing ejection and suspension penalties for fighting, a fairly dramatic change from the attitude of the NHL's former commissioner, John Ziegler, who claimed that " spontaneous fighting was a 'justifiable outlet for the frustrations of hockey'."[20] Indeed, it was due to articles by a number of sports journalists and writers that the NHL finally abandoned its advocacy of fighting as necessary violence and began accepting more socially responsible official positions as regards excessive violence. *Sports Illustrated*, for instance, began calling for "an automatic five-game suspension whenever a player dropped his gloves or swung his stick, and a ten game suspension if he did it again."[21]

e. Control the marketing of violence

If, as Christopher Lasch maintains, "commercialization has turned play into work, subordinated the athlete's pleasure to the spectator's, and reduced the spectator himself to a state of passivity,"[22] the level of violence we currently see in professional sport may be unavoidable without making some attempt to control that commercialization. Certainly, when videos of the most devastating football and hockey hits are sold on ESPN between periods of hockey games or on *Sports Center* between footage of that day's most violent hits, it is clear that marketing has gotten out of control.

Moreover, the selling of violence is a management decision that comes from the top, from sports' highest echelons of management. Thus, only a few years ago, the dominant sentiment in the National Hockey League was that violence, *as long as it sold*, was acceptable. A perfect example of this commercialized management attitude toward violence can be heard in John Ziegler's response to being asked about the brutal play of the penalty-leading Philadelphia Flyers in the early 1980s. The NHL league president answered defensively about the Flyers' frequently offensive behavior: "'If the other twenty teams were as successful, I'd be pleased, regardless of how they achieved such success'."[23]

Violence sold in the early 1980s but, by the latter part of the decade, with attendance down and national television contracts in the balance, hockey violence stopped selling quite so well, and more stringent anti-fighting penalties were instituted. And these penalties have worked, at least to some extent, in reducing the brawls that had come to mark so many hockey games.

One obvious conclusion can fairly be drawn from hockey's experience with selling violence: a decision by upper management to stop promoting the violence in their sport can lead to a significant diminution of unnecessary and injurious violence in the games. Indeed, unless top management sees that selling violence will ultimately adversely affect their bottom line, as hockey belatedly and partially has begun to do, there is no chance that violence in professional sport will diminish to acceptable levels.

Beyond the leagues' official responses to violence are their responses, or non-responses, to the selling of violence in their names. When they have any legal rights to prevent selling such products as videos that glorify the most violent aspects of their sport, they should exercise those rights. Even when they have no veto power over selling violence in their names, the top league executives should loudly and publicly eschew such commercialized violence. The correct attitude for the health of professional sport, as cited earlier, is National League President Coleman's reply that he intended to put a stop to brawls because "it's not good for baseball."[24]

Legal remedies to curb violence

Legal remedies to curbing beyond the rules violence in professional sports are certainly controversial, as an ESPN program first aired in July of 1994, and rebroadcast in March of 1995, underscored. In terms of public opinion as to whether legal action should be brought against players who hurt one another in beyond the rules violence, 53% thought such legal action to be justified, at least sometimes, while 47% did not.[25]

As this television program suggested, a great many people feel that sports exist outside of the normal legal and moral codes of ordinary life. The violence that goes on within the boundaries of the game simply does not connect in many fans' minds to the violence that they might experience once they walk out of the stadium or arena, and athletes are somehow intrinsically different from the mugger who accosts them as they walk to their car after the game.

Furthermore, using the legal system to control on the field, court, or rink violence can have unanticipated repercussions. For instance, the ESPN program, "Our Violent Games," cited the case of one minor league hockey player who was injured by police while being arrested for an on-the-ice incident. Do we want to incite crowds by allowing the police to arrest players in full view of fans, particularly given the proclivity of some police to be unnecessarily rough when performing their duties? To exaggerate only slightly, might specialized police training in sports arrests be required for all arena police agencies?

Undeniably, the question of how and when the legal system should become involved in sports violence needs to be addressed, for despite many people's reticence to include sports stars within the normal course of legal responsibility, our system of government is partly premised on the notion that everyone is equal under the law. If we are to exempt professional sports from legal responsibility for their beyond the rules actions, do we not implicitly undermine the rule of law?

At least three levels of the legal/enforcement system need to be considered when discussing the law and sports violence: (a) the individual legal responsibility that players, coaches, and clubs may have for injuries to opposing players; (b) the possible need to legislate against violence at a national, Congressional level; and (c) the continuing need for professional sports to do a more socially responsible job of self-enforcement against excess violence. In the following sections, I address these concerns.

a. *Individual legal responsibilities*

When beyond the rules violence (and sometimes even inside the rules violence) results in serious injury to a player, whose fault, legally and morally, is the injury? Of course, the courts ultimately determine legal culpability in individual cases, and the state and national legislatures can guide the court's decisions by passing laws relevant to violence in sports. But to what extent should the major sports organizations stand in the way of the normal legal remedies? And how much are the clubs and the leagues responsible for career-ending and crippling injuries, given their often slack enforcement of rules and their complicity in creating an atmosphere where violence is tolerated, if not actually encouraged?

As discussed in chapter 3, violence has been a tricky problem since the advent of professional sports. Today, with contracts worth millions of dollars at stake, players, coaches, and clubs all have elementary greed feeding into their desire to win at all costs and, because of this, to some extent they are all jointly responsible for the state of their sports. As Underwood maintains:

> When athletes are desperate to succeed, to get to where all that money is, and stay there for awhile, they do whatever they have to do. When coaches are put in a desperate win-or-else situation, they are not likely to look askance at intimidation and violence if those things can help

keep them employed. This, in turn, has led to the worst part of the equation: the insane tolerance of an epidemic injury rate . . . The bottom-line mentalities who control sport at the top have a lot to answer for in this regard.[26]

But what happens when one player violently and quite intentionally assaults another in an incident that is clearly beyond the rules, causing the other player grievous injury? In one of the most famous cases, that of Kermit Washington's 1977 on-the-court mugging of Rudy Tomjanovich, an incident that in any other venue would have resulted in battery charges, mug shots, and possible jail time, no legal charges were filed. Washington was suspended for 60 days from the NBA and given a $10,000 fine. Moreover, the personal injury lawsuit that Tomjanovich pressed, and eventually won,[27] was against the ownership of Kermit Washington's team, the Los Angeles Lakers, not against the player.

Since the assault was witnessed by many people, both the thousands at the game and the millions who watched replays on television, there was no doubt that the assault merited charges. After all, Tomjanovich's face was shattered by the blow Washington struck, several reconstructive surgeries were required, and Tomjanovich's career entered a prolonged hiatus. Moreover, the influence that such brutal actions might have had on viewers, particularly young ones, is inestimable. That is to say, if the legal system does not want to glorify violence, should it not prosecute those who exercise clearly illegal violence before the enormous audiences that television and huge arenas provide to the professional athlete?

There are potential problems with bringing assault charges to trial based on incidents in professional sport. Many, perhaps almost all, injuries occur in the heat of competition and determining intentionality may be as difficult as determining a flagrant foul under the current NBA rules. What appears on television replay to be a hard, but within the normal parameters of the game, foul may get slapped with a flagrant by a quick-whistling official who wants to control the tenor of the game's violent edge.

However, although most incidents on a field, court, or rink are not good candidates for criminal action, the most brutal incidents, in my opinion, should be prosecuted, perhaps automatically, according to laws modeled on some states' domestic violence regulations that put the decision to prosecute in the hands of legal authorities rather than in the hands of an abused spouse who may be so intimidated by a violent partner that she (or he) refuses to press charges, despite broken bones or massive bruises.

So, too, a player may be intimidated from pursuing criminal charges against a criminal attack by an opposing player, even though the assault may have taken place with a hockey stick or a baseball bat and may have left the assaulted player seriously or permanently injured. The peer pressure from other players and from club ownership and management not to press charges certainly must work to suppress at least some legitimate cases against particularly brutal attackers. Thus, allowing the legal system to press charges independent of the assaulted player, should be encouraged in cases where there have been serious violations of basic standards of ethical behavior on the playing field.

That is, when a baseball player intentionally coldcocks another with a bat, as Juan Marichal, the San Francisco Giant pitcher, once did to the Los Angeles Dodger catcher, John Roseboro, society cannot afford to treat the crime differently than it would treat such an incident in a store, factory, university, or workplace. If a line worker at an automobile manufacturing plant takes a tire iron to his co-worker, the legal system is supposed to intervene with criminal proceedings. Kermit Washington might not have been convicted of any criminal worngdoing for his assault on Tomjanovich, for a jury or judge might have found his "I-thought-he-was-coming-at-me" defense credible, but he should have been brought to court. To allow such blatant incidents to become invisible in terms of criminal culpability sends an unacceptable message to young people.

For those who aim at becoming a professional athlete, it appears that punishment does not apply to crimes committed during the course of their professional work life, and this inevitably will have the effect of adding to the mindset of thuggery that affects too many athletes on and off the court.

Beyond a doubt, in their pursuit of million dollar or more contracts, many aspiring young athletes will push the intimidation factor to, and beyond, its limit. If they see that the limit allows what would, off the playing field, be criminal behavior, at least some of them will engage in imitative behavior of the injuriously high-stick swinger or the bat-wielding, beaned hitter. The child (cited in Chapter 1 of this book) who asked, "When exactly are you supposed to charge the mound,"[28] needs to understand that the absolutely correct answer is "never," and certainly not with bat in hand, lest you be treated as an accused criminal, read your Miranda rights in front of the gathered crowd, and hauled off to the local magistrate or jail.

It may be that the issue of fame and legal responsibility has become much murkier, due to the fact that people think of their athletic heroes as above the law. That is, it is unclear as to how carefully people want individual athletes to have to adhere to the normal social and legal conventions which apply to the rest of American citizens. Thus, when the boxer, Mike Tyson, was convicted of rape and sent to prison, a great many of his admirers excused his behavior and said he was being wrongfully punished. The O.J. Simpson murder trial also raises issues of how we think of sports heroes in relation to the law. However, regardless of Simpson's individual guilt or innocence, too often we maintain one set of standards for our neighbor's behavior and another for a sports star's behavior, often to the detriment of both the star and our own sense of values. For instance, when Mickey Mantle's drinking was part of his baseball hero's persona, a great many people thought he was merely acting in the macho way sports heroes are supposed to act; only when he went into an alcohol rehabilitation program and the press reported on the terrible difficulties Mantle had experienced as a result of alcoholism did some of the public's double standard fade.

To those who do not aspire to becoming professional athletes, the message may seem to be that money and position in society protects the successful athlete from the laws and liabilities of less privileged people. This perception can only reinforce the class and economic barriers that have created so much unnecessary divisiveness in American society. When non-athletes see the law of the street, where anything goes in terms of violence, taken into the stadiums, how can we expect them to respect the rule of law? Indeed, it is hypocritical, at least in the most flagrant cases, for society to automatically exculpate an individual from legal responsibility for acts of violence merely because that person was playing a game at the time of the violation. Intent and actions, not occupation, ought to be the deciding factors as to whether prosecutors prefer criminal charges.

A recent example of how the judicial system should look at intentional harm done on a playing field can be found in Great Britain where soccer players have been getting sentenced to jail for the worst of their violent antics. The local magistrate, Sheriff Alexander Eccles, was quite explicit about his reasons for jailing the offender.

> Everton striker, Duncan Ferguson, was sentenced to three months in jail yesterday in Glasgow for headbutting an opponent during a soccer match . . . Ferguson, 23, was found guilty after a two-day trial earlier this month.

Ferguson is the third soccer player in Britain sentenced to jail this year for violent incidents. Noting that it was Ferguson's third conviction, Eccles said he was jailing the player 'both in the public interest' and to emphasize to him that such behavior could not be tolerated. He noted that Ferguson was in a prominent position as a player, looked up to by young people.[29]

Although jailing three players within a six-month period may seem excessive to many people who routinely accept beyond the rules violence as an integral part of professional sport, such actions are essential if we are to reassert a sense of ethical order to the worst aspects of violence in American professional sport. Three months in jail is certainly not out of line with what a three-time convicted assaulter might get in an American court. Indeed, many people would think three months for a third assault conviction to be rather lenient.

b. Legislation concerning sports violence

There have been periodic Congressional efforts to look into the need to legislate rules concerning violence in professional sports, one of the most widely publicized of which was the failed *1983 Sports Violence Arbitration Act.* Proposed by Representative Ron Mottl (D-Ohio), this act would have empowered Congress "to set up arbitration boards to make judgments and impose fines from league to league."[30] The Federal government, in other words, would have forced management to be liable for the violations of its players and would have assumed control of the punishment process. Also, the bill provided hefty penalties: "a fine of not more than $5,000, imprisonment of not more than a year, or both—for the use of 'excessive physical force' in professional sports events."[31]

The idea that the Federal government can act as a policing agency for professional sports did not impress Congress sufficiently to pass the bill, and the utility of such legislation can certainly be questioned from both a social and a legal point of view. Indeed, treating crimes on the athletic field as needing additional penalties to those already prescribed by the Federal, state, and local legal codes makes the same error as treating acts of overt, intentional, beyond the rules violence as acceptable in professional sports. That is to say, they somehow are considered to be outside the normal jurisdictional boundaries.

Perhaps the experience of the Federal negotiator, William Usery, in the recent baseball strike best illustrates the difficulties the Federal government is likely to have if they involve themselves in the administration of professional sports. For Mr. Usery, a negotiator of renowned skills, the experience proved to be a low point professionally, as it was clear he could do little to move the negotiations forward. Moreover, whatever political will there previously might have been to regulate professional sports through legislative means proved to be minimal, as Congress could not even agree to talk about baseball's anti-trust exemption.

c. *Professional sports' self-policing*

Rather than rely on Congress to be the law-maker of last resort, professional sport increasingly is choosing to police itself more carefully, to develop more stringent and enforceable regulations, and to talk a less stridently violence-oriented advertising talk. But there is a substantial distance that professional sports leagues can still go to make a too violent situation much less so.

One alternative, explored by Chris J. Carlson in the *Southern California Law Review*, concerns holding the player's club responsible for malicious injuries to players from opposing teams. In addition to fines and suspensions, Carlson suggests that:

> The offending player's club should be made (1) to pay the salary of the injured player during his convalescence, (2) to pay his medical expenses, (3) to pay compensatory damages if he is unable to play in the future, (4) to pay fines for failing to control its own player's actions, and (5) to pay damages or relinquish draft choices to the injured player's club for the loss of his services.[32]

Of course, it would be impossible for clubs to agree on such a system, unless they were convinced it was in their own best interests. While Carlson advocated Congressional intervention via legislation as the way to force club owners into such a plan, Underwood's suspicion of such government intervention is well-grounded. However, the stricter rules, especially the ones in hockey penalizing coaches and clubs for fighting, suggests that there is a level of violence that has become unacceptable and that leagues will do what is necessary to control that excessive violence.

It was, arguably, the lure of a major television contract that prompted the NHL to crack down on the worst of the on-the-rink violence through enforcing stricter rules about fighting. Similarly, for the NBA, it was partly spectacles like the New York Knicks' Derek Harper wrestling an opposing player into the stands during a nationally-televised playoff game in 1994, practically at Commissioner David Stern's feet, that finally got the NBA to strengthen its anti-fighting responses. In 1995, throughout the league, there has been a tighter enforcement of regulations than were enacted before the 1995 season. In both the NHL and the NBA, the fear of losing the public's television interest may have a considerable degree of clout in making the leagues more responsive to the need to control violence in their sports.

One fairly simple, but potentially effective way that the professional sports leagues can use to help change their image from one of no-holds-barred violence to one of within-the-rules play is to engage in extended public relations campaigns through the media, television in particular. That is, since television is the medium through which professional sports have gained much of their audience, the leagues can use public service announcements to counteract the poisonous images of violence transmitted by replays of vicious high sticks, intentionally flagrant fouls, and beanball brawls.

A model for such public announcement spots aired during the 1995 NBA playoffs. This thirty second spot featured the New York Knicks center, Patrick Ewing, who narrated a brief scene from his youth. He related that, as a teenager, he had moved to a new city, Boston, and the students there had not been as peaceful as his contemporaries in Jamaica had been. On the screen, there is a scene of a young Ewing being confronted by a troublemaker in the hall. Instead of fighting, however, Ewing relates that he walked away from the potential fight. The public relations spot finishes with Ewing speaking directly to the young people who are watching the playoff game to walk away from fights. "Peace," Ewing says at the fadeout, flashing the "V" sign with his fingers.

This spot is effective in communicating an antiviolence message, partly because Patrick Ewing, as a former "Dream Team" member, is one of the most recognizable athletes in the NBA, and he has the reputation of being a fearless warrior and an intimidating basketball presence. And, because the spot focused on Ewing's real life personality, and not on his Olympian stature among the NBA's elite, it speaks directly to youth who might find themselves in similar situations, whether or not they are basketball players with a reputation to protect.

The other professional sports would do well to emulate this public relations spot by the NBA, perhaps even speaking directly to on-the-rink or field violence. Certainly, having someone of the stature of Deion Sanders or Reggie White explain the difference between a legal hit and a dangerously illegal one might enlighten some high school players as to the potential injuries that can be inflicted by a player intent on bending the spirit and letter of the rules. Similarly, getting an Eric Lindros or Wayne Gretzky to speak up about the excessive violence in hockey or about how to play hockey without having to resort to stick or fist swinging, might go at least a worthwhile distance in changing the habits of younger players. Moreover, although such public service announcements would have little immediate effect on changing the climate of uncontrolled violence that affects all of the major professional team sports in America, eventually some of the kids watching the spots will become professional hockey players or football players themselves, and their behavior on the field will inevitably be affected by the positive messages they absorbed in their younger years.

The leagues might even supplement the fines and suspensions they levy on violent offenders with a sort of "community service" provision, modeled on the judicial system, whereby to regain playing privileges, the offending player must work directly with the violence that his action perhaps encourages. That is, the leagues could require players to make public service announcements aimed at curbing just the sort of actions that got the player suspended and fined. Or the player might be directed toward other, appropriate community service work, possibly directly with youthful athletes. In addition to counteracting their negative influence on others, such announcements might have the occasional effect of getting the player himself to review his attitude toward injuring others.

There are no panaceas to the problem of beyond the rules violence, and public service announcements by themselves are hardly more than a palliative. Nevertheless, if combined with tough enforcement of existing rules and institution of other measures to control violence, such announcements can produce a worthwhile effect. Gradually, perhaps over the course of a generation, players will come to accept these measures as vital to the health and popularity of their sport, and the frequency and severity of beyond the rules violence will subside.

Notes

1. Richard E. Leakey, *The Making of Mankind* (New York: E.P. Dutton, 1981), p. 219.
2. Raymond Dart, "The predatory transition from ape to man," in R.E. Leakey, *The Making of Mankind* (New York: E.P. Dutton, 1981), p. 221.
3. Desmond Morris, "Altruistic Behavior,' in *Manwatching: A Field Guide to Human Behavior* (New York: Harry Abrams, 1977).
4. Loren Eisley, *The Unexpected Universe* (New York, Harcourt, Brace & World, 1969), p. 95.
5. Ashley Montagu, *Learning Non-Aggression* (New York: Oxford University Press, 1978), p. 3.
6. Jacob Bronowski, *The Ascent of Man* (Boston: Little, Brown, 1973), p. 88.
7. Montagu, p. 4.
8. The concepts of the global village and the shrinking distances between cultures is intelligently discussed by Alvin Toffler in several of his books, including *Future Shock* (1973) and *The Third Wave* (1980).
9. Jane Roberts, *The Nature of the Psyche* (Englewood Cliffs, NJ: Prentice-Hall, 1979), pp. 186-187.
10. Paul Reps, ed., *Zen Flesh, Zen Bones* (Rutland, VT: Charles E. Tuttle, 1990), pp. 86-87.
11. Montagu, p. 5.
12. Montagu, p. 6.
13. Michener, p. 428.
14. Fawcett and Thomas, p. 395.
15. George Vecsey, "First Off, Calm Down Noise and Mascots." *The New York Times*, February 12, 1995, p. 2S.
16. Vecsey, February 12, 1995.
17. Sally Jenkins, "Persona Non Grata." *Sports Illustrated*, August 23, 1993, p. 32.
18. John Underwood, p. 82.
19. Underwood, p. 88.
20. Underwood, p. 91.
21. Underwood, p. 93.
22. Christopher Lasch, "The Degradation of Sport," in *Philosophic Inquiry in Sport*, William J. Morgan and Klaus V. Meier, eds. Champaign, IL: Human Kinetics Publishers, 1988, p. 404.
23. Underwood, p. 91.
24. Hal Bodley, "NL Boss Takes Hard Line on Outbreak of Brawling." *USA Today*, May 6, 1994, p. 6C.
25. ESPN. "Our Violent Games," *Outside the Lines*. March 23, 1995.
26. Underwood, pp. 84-85.

27. Tomjanovich won $1.8 million in actual damages and another $1.5 million in punitive damages against California Sports, Inc., the Lakers' corporate owners.

28. Hal Bodley, "NL Boss Takes Hard Line on Outbreak of Brawling." *USA Today*, May 6, 1994, p. 6C.

29. *New York Times*, "Player Sent to Jail for a Head Butt." May 26, 1995, p. B-12.

30. Underwood, p. 97.

31. Underwood, p. 82.

32. Underwood, p. 96.

Chapter 5

ℰℭ

A New Paradigm for Controlling Violence

Introduction

O ther cultures than our own look at the body/soul debate in quite different terms than our lineage that extends from the Greeks through Aquinas and Descartes, to Darwin, Freud, and other scientific rationalists. In Zen Buddhism, for instance, although existence itself may be an illusion, it is all a unitary and quite real illusion, body and soul as manifestations of the same energy source. Thus, the thrust of the following teaching story is that reality, which involves both body and soul, is as close as a whack from a master.

Yamaoka Tesshu, as a young student of Zen, visited one master after another. He called upon Dokuon of Shokoku.

Desiring to show his attainment, he said: 'The mind, Buddha, and sentient beings, after all, do not exist. The true nature of phenomena is emptiness. There is no realization, no delusion, no sage, no mediocrity. There is no giving and nothing to be received.'

Dokuon, who was smoking quietly, said nothing. Suddenly he whacked Yamaoka with his bamboo pipe. This made the youth quite angry.

'If nothing exists,' inquired Dokuon, 'where did this anger come from?'[1]

The mind and the body are not merely connected, as a motor might be connected to a chassis; rather, they are different manifestations of the same thing, of energy. Moreover, there is a constant interplay between what we call "physical" and what we refer to as "spiritual," and it is not so simple as the cause and effect postulated by Plato. A whack with a bamboo pipe elicits both a physical and a spiritual response, and these responses cannot be easily untangled from one another, for in the Buddhist tradition, there are no essential differences between body and mind.

It is a basic premise of Japanese and Chinese martial arts that "refinement of the body is inseparable from refinement of the mind,"[2] and the philosophical bent of the martial arts can be useful in understanding how to alter the current climate of escalating violence in professional sports, as well as in society in general.

As R. Scott Kretchmer wrote in his 1983 article, "Ethics and Sport": "Metaphysical understanding must precede ethical prescription."[3]   In this chapter, alternative ways of looking at the body/soul debate, in the context of its relevance to the issue of violence in professional sports, are discussed.   These alternative perspectives emerge from metaphysical principles elucidated by Zen and Chinese Buddhist teachings and practices, some of them adapted to Western culture by a number of writers, including Timothy Gallwey, John Curtis, Ron Sieh, Shi Ming, and Shinobu Abe.

In the following sections, I first offer three extended analogies that elucidate the nature of the retraining task involved in weaning professional athletics from an over-dependence on beyond the rules violence. Then I discuss points at which the philosophy of the East is coming into more use by athletes and how some of the ideas even of Western science are slowly flowing toward an acceptance of a profound connection between mind and body that implicitly rejects the excesses of scientific positivism.

Three Analogies: Drunken Driving, Smoking, Drugs

There is no doubt that ethical issues can be taught to the members of a culture, and eliminating excessive aggression in professional sport is at least partly an ethical issue. That is, reducing beyond the rules violence deals with training athletes in a set of principles and moral values.

In the 1980s, after decades of carnage on America's highways due to drunken driving, society finally made a more or less concerted effort to reduce the injuries and fatalities connected to alcohol's consumption by drivers. A combination of increased penalties for drunken driving, the expansion of responsibility for drunken driving to establishments that serve alcohol to the public, increased enforcement activities, and substantially increased public education efforts seem to be working, in the sense that alcohol-related traffic accidents and fatalities are decreasing.

Smoking, another recognized public health hazard, has also begun to lessen as a threat due to the many public health campaigns fought over it since the scientific connection between smoking and disease was made more than three decades ago. It is so much tougher to smoke now than it was in the 1950s, at least in terms of smoking's social standing, that a great many people have quit and others never started. Beginning with the ban on cigarette advertising on television in the late 1960s, and continuing with the warning labels on cigarette packages and print advertisements, through the auspices of the Surgeon General's office in Washington, the federal government has discouraged smoking.[4]

Of course, there are still a great many alcohol-related deaths on our highways, and there are still many smokers who die of lung cancer or other smoking-related illnesses. Nevertheless, over the course of time, serious attempts to reduce the level of drunken driving and the prevalence of smoking have paid off in a lower percentage of fatalities and smoking-related illnesses across the population. It is simply not as acceptable today to smoke or to drink and drive as it used to be; that is, our cultural training is changing, and we are seeing progress in bringing society toward a more responsible attitude toward these health and welfare-related ethical issues.

Similarly, we do not allow professional athletes to use performance-enhancement drugs, including steroids, cocaine, or a variety of quite legal medications for such conditions as asthma. Although too many athletes still risk banishment for using steroids, for instance, thinking they can fool the drug tests through a variety of clever strategies, the increased international vigilance about drug testing, and publicity about the drugs' side effects and their long-term health hazards have certainly decreased their usage at the highest levels of sport.

A serious attempt to retrain athletes concerning the ethics and efficacy of beyond the rules violence could be effective, just as have been the cases with retraining segments of our society to smoke less, stop drinking when driving, and stop using performance enhancing, but illegal or unsafe, drugs. To recall what Ashley Montagu said about stopping violent aggression: "human beings can learn virtually anything."[5]

Appropriate and thorough mental conditioning is required for athletes to control beyond the rules violence, and yet little effort is devoted to training mental aspects of competition. As John Curtis maintains, "most athletes spend 90-95% of their time on the development of physical skills and very little time on the development of mental factors that lead to athletic success."[6] Part of the necessary mental retraining, particularly for athletes at the highest skill levels, involves how to re-connect the mind and the body in ways discouraged by the many centuries of separating mind and body in the philosophic and cultural history of the West. In this regard, certain of the Eastern martial arts present a wealth of philosophic and practical retraining possibilities.

East Meets West

Introduction

Especially in the years after World War II, virtually no world-renowned scientist was willing to publicly take scientific positivism to task for the way in which it separates mind and body. Then, in Thomas Hanna's words, in accepting the 1981 Nobel Prize, the American psychologist, Roger Sperry, laid "the foundation for an authentic science of responsibility."[7]

> The events of inner experience, as emergent properties of brain processes, become themselves explanatory causal constructs in their own right, interacting at their own level with their own laws and dynamics. The whole world of inner experience (the world of the humanities) long rejected by 20th century scientific materialism thus becomes recognized and included with the domain of science.[8]

The rejection of scientific materialism by the scientific community is certainly not a generalizable phenomenon, for it is still the dominant paradigm in our culture. Moreover, even if the leading edge of such fields as physics increasingly recognizes the unity of mind and body, the conception of such unity within the beliefs of most people is bound to lag many years or decades behind.[9] Nevertheless, as with changing people's attitudes about smoking or wearing seat belts, attitudes can and do change over time. In this regard, several concepts extracted from the founder of the Japanese martial art of Aikido, Morihei Uyeshiba, present a starting point. In the next section, Uyeshiba's basic concept of mind/body unity, translated into its relevance to competitive sports, is outlined. Then, Shi Ming's philosophy of the higher martial arts is explicated as a further elaboration of some of Uyeshiba's principles.

Morihei Uyeshiba's Zen unity

There is a nice irony to the fact that Zen Buddhism, which emphasizes inner peace, should be a focus for many of the Chinese and Japanese martial arts. How is it that a physical activity which comes from an essentially military tradition can be best practiced by someone at peace within him or her self?

In the following four subsections (a-d), I first (a) give a history of Aikido, a modern martial art, founded by Uyeshiba Morihei (1883-1968), partly in response to what he felt was lacking in the traditional martial arts. Then, I discuss the central issues of compassion and non-competition within the Aikido tradition. Then (c), I discuss Uyeshiba's "Path to Selflessness," principally based on the brief but excellent discussion of it in Olson and Comfort (1986). Finally, (d), I discuss the implications from Aikkdo in terms of what Paul Linden calls "learning how to learn."

a. The beginnings of Aikido

Uyeshiba Morihei was born in a family that had a long tradition of samurai warriors in his family and, as he was the only son of his parents' five children, he received formal physical training in sumo wrestling and swimming from an early age. However, since he was of short stature, barely five feet tall as an adult, and as he was rather sickly as a child, he did not take up any athletic endeavor seriously until he was well into his teens. Indeed, it was only after a bout with beriberi at the age of 19, and an initial rejection by the military service, that he began to exercise more seriously. When he finally was allowed into the military, he prospered and earned a martial arts teaching license after four years. Thus, largely through willing and working himself into excellent physical condition, Uyeshiba accomplished the first step in his creation of a new form of martial arts.[10]

For several years after leaving the military, Uyeshiba and his family lived a hard life as settlers in the remote province of Hokkaido, returning to his hometown only after the death of his father, and later settling in

Ayabe as a disciple of the new Omoto-kyo religion, which was "a mixture of Shinto mythology, shamanism, faith-healing, and personality cult."[11] Within the context of this religion, Uyeshiba began the process of calming his mind and his often hot temper under the auspices of the cult's leader, Onisaburo. Moreover, since Onisaburo was a pacifist, and Morihei Uyeshiba was a martial arts teacher, there seemingly would have been a contradiction between their beliefs. However, as John Stevens explains, this was not the case.

> Onisaburo was an advocate of nonviolent resistance and universal disarmament who once said, 'Armament and war are the means by which landlords and capitalists make their profit, while the poor must suffer; there is nothing in the world more harmful than war and more foolish than armament.' Why did he welcome the martial artist Morihei, building a dojo for him . . . ? Onisaburo realized that Morihei's purpose on earth was 'to teach the real meaning of budo: an end to all fighting and contention.'[12]

By 1927, Uyeshiba had broken with Onisaburo and had set up his own dojo in Tokyo. Although Uyeshiba seems to have supported the Japanese Imperial government in World War II, his son, Kisshomaru, indicated that Morihei harbored grave doubts about the Japanese cause, and his former religious mentor's pacifist beliefs certainly affected the manner in which he developed Aikido. Before the end of the war, anticipating a tremendous Japanese defeat, he moved to the prefecture of Iwami where he completed the development of Aikido, refining and improving the martial art until his death in 1969.

While there is no fixed form in Aikido, and thus there are a number of schools teaching variants of Uyeshiba's techniques, the basic premise of all schools is simple: "real budo," Shirata Rinjiro states, "is to learn how to live, how to live together with others in harmony and peace."[13] Indeed, "the motto of Aikido training is *Masakatsu Akatsu*, 'By acting in accordance with the truth we always emerge victorious'."[14] Moreover, there are a number of basic tenets to all schools of Aikido, and these are outlined in the following sections.

b. Compassion and non-competition

The reconciliation of the irony of needing inner peace to successfully practice Aikido lies in the fact that what in the West might be viewed as the "enemy" is, according to Zen thinking, viewed as the "opponent."

This view of one's opponent is accomplished by nurturing two vital character traits so often missing, or opposite, in the West: compassion and noncompetitiveness. While the idea of a compassionate, noncompetitive American professional sport might seem to be a contradiction in terms, the way in which Aikido practices compassionate noncompetitiveness is not at all in contradiction to accomplishing athletic excellence and superiority. As George Leonard noted, for Aikido, Vince Lombardi's dictum that "winning isn't everything; it's the only thing," would be changed to "winning isn't everything; it's one element in the dance."[15]

Aikido, as a practice, emphasizes the nature of choice, of free-will, in that its practitioner chooses how to view an attack. Compassion allows to *aikidoka* to choose an appropriate mode of defense. As Olson and Comfort explain:

> Physically, the techniques may lie anywhere on a continuum from not touching to totally devastating an attacker. Philosophically speaking, this provides . . . a wide range of choices in dealing with a violent attack. The fact that there are choices suggests another continuum in regards to a philosophy of defense. At the upper end of the spectrum lies the choice of compassion, whereby the aikidoka chooses to meet an intended violent attack with love, harmonizes with the aggressor, neutralizes the attack . . . The other end of the spectrum holds the choice for complete disregard for human life. . . . Uyeshiba saw love as the heart of martial arts in which harmony instead of resistance . . . [was] practiced.[16]

The emphasis on choice means that the practitioner of Aikido is faced with both a choice of techniques and a choice of philosophy. However, assuming the attitude that the opponent is not the enemy can still produce intense effort, to which George Leonard, a *aikidoka* himself, attests.

> Aikido, one of the most dancelike of sports, forbids competition . . . Yet even here an attacker is required to create the dance. Every akidoist faces the problem of finding a good practice partner, one who will attack with real intent. The greatest gift the akidoist can receive from a partner is the clean, true attack, the blow that, unless blocked or avoided, will strike home with real effect . . . The halfhearted, off-target attack is harder to deal with and more likely to lead to injury.[17]

Aikido does not deny the reality of violence; indeed, it is still, in its essence, a martial art. Rather, it metaphorically treats violence as a dance with nonviolence, two opposites engaged in making a harmonious whole, not unlike the Taoist yin and yang. "The power of the dancing Shiva," Leonard reminds us, drawing from Hinduism, "is that it shows us the dancer of destruction and the dancer of creation joined in a single body, dancing to sustain the world."[18]

One Western advocate of compassion as a motivating force in professional athletics is the basketball coach, Pat Riley, coach of the Miami Heat, as of this writing, and former three-time world champion coach of the 1980s Los Angeles Lakers. Riley consciously uses anger as a motivational device for his team, regarding anger as an "art" that requires advance planning, great timing, and exquisite sensitivity. It also requires something else: "Compassion is vital. Without it, anger degenerates into brutality...."[19]

As was suggested in the Leonard quote about the value of finding a good Aikido practice partner, noncompetitiveness does not mean lack of effort. Rather, because "the aikidoka trains toward a perfection of the self,"[20] the opponent is regarded as an essential part of the process of testing oneself and one's progress. While Aikido is, in this sense, not a competitive sport, the attitude that the opponents are actually essential parts of a cooperative endeavor at maximizing the athletes' skills can help the individual hone his focus on further developing his physical skills.

c. The path of selflessness

In accordance with Zen practice, Uyeshiba's invention of Aikido includes three levels of self-awareness, all of which must be mastered by the adept: Zen skin, Zen flesh, and Zen bones. As these names imply, with each level, one gets closer to the center of the art of Aikido.

Zen skin, the *Kihon Waza*, constitute the basic foundation techniques of Aikido. As in learning any conventional sport, the idea is to build up a basic vocabulary of movement through practice and repetition, as well as through study and analysis. This stage of learning is essential, although eventually the aikidoka must reach beyond such an analytical, "scientific" approach. Indeed, in all sports, particularly at the professional level, the foundation techniques are generally well in place and, though practice and repetition is still essential to maintain one's competitive sharpness, going past this learning is routine.

Zen flesh, the second level of an Aikido practitioner's attainment, involves "learning to see and feel the rhythm of movement." Moreover, as Olson and Comfort point out:

> The underlying foundation of all movement, particularly the martial arts, is correct breathing. The correct breathing process produces a rhythm that is analogous to a rhythmic flow of energy. Inhaling, drawing air in, is seen as a drawing of energy from the surroundings into the akidoka's center; exhaling, expelling air out, is viewed as an extension of directed energy from the akidoka's center back into the environment. This energy, with its close connection to breathing and an individual's center, is referred to in the martial arts as *ki*. Through the experience and understanding of the rhythm of breathing (the flow of energy) comes the understanding of the rhythm of movement of energy flow within an attack.[21]

The unity of this way of thinking is everywhere evident. Indeed, for a person firmly committed to the scientific-rationalist approach to reality, the very concept of the rhythm of one's breathing reflecting larger synchronicities (to use Jung's word loosely[22]) would be unthinkable. However, the idea that one's breathing is released energy is quite an old one in the Zen and pre-Zen traditions of China, perhaps originating in the 13th century, reputedly by a Taoist monk, Chang Sang-feng, the founder of the martial art of T'ai Chi Ch'uan.

> The story has it that T'ai Chi was revealed to Chang during a noon-time meditation. Looking out of the window, he saw a magpie trying to attack a snake. The snake teased the bird, managing always to be just out of reach, curling around and around in spirals, as snakes are wont to do. Thus the essence of T'ai Chi—the inviolate nature of the circle.[23]

The dance, simultaneously one of breath and of body, is done in imitation of the snake, the focus entirely on the present moment, on the attacking magpie, yet it is done with a degree of playfulness, of teasing. While the analogy, of course, does not pertain to professional sports in all circumstances, certainly the attitude developed in training the body within the T'ai Chi Ch'uan and Aikido traditions, with their emphasis on the interconnectedness of inner and outer worlds through the breath and its energy, can be of great value. Not only would this value be in training the athlete's body and mind to properly focus on the athletic objective, the attitude of the athlete towards others can be gradually and subtly changed to better reflect the societal and administrative aims of controlling the violence on the playing field, court, or rink to reflect acceptable values.

The third level of awareness in Uyeshiba's system of Aikido, Zen bones, unites the dancer and the dance in a unique manner. "At this level of attainment...the attack and the defense, the mind and the body, no longer exist as separate entities; there is only the harmony of the pattern of movement."[24]

Even without formal training in the martial arts or in Eastern metaphysical approaches, the best athletes often manifest quite similar thinking and training to what Uyeshiba advocates. When Michael Jordan soars toward the basket, when Cal Ripkin dives for a ball in the hole, when Jerry Rice twists backward to catch a touchdown pass, the dance and the dancer are one, as they are in an Aikido master's movements. Indeed, before O.J. Simpson was made even more famous by his double murder trial, George Leonard maintained that "the whole complex structure of pro football was created primarily so that O.J. (and others like him) can dance." Leonard continues, expanding the dance/Aikido analogy to include the entire structure of professional football:

> To dance, O.J. needs worthy teammates and effective coaches. He also needs worthy opponents; it is, in fact, their excellence and their full commitment to stop him that forces his dance to higher levels. He needs a physical and psychological context for his dance—thus, the stadium, the business organization, the public-relations and ticket sales efforts, the officials, and, finally, the fans, the collusion of all involved to make each game and each season into something dramatic and significant.[25]

An athlete at the level of Simpson in his prime may play for the money, but once in the game, only the game exists, the mind and body operating as one with the dance of the game. While even most professional athletes may not reach such an inner state, using Zen bones as a goal of training will alter the focus of using mere intimidation that a great many professional athletes tout.

Of course, the Path of Selflessness fits in quite well with the concept of team play. Pat Riley, for instance, writes of what he calls "the Disease of Me," and how it can undermine even the best of basketball teams unless a sense of selflessness can be restored. "Willing sacrifice is the great paradox," Riley writes. "You must give up something in the immediate present—comfort, ease, recognition, quick rewards—to attract something even better in the future: a full heart and a sense that you did something which counted."26

d. Learning how to learn

Until medical science began seriously examining the connections between smoking and lung cancer, among other diseases, the American public bought into the cigarette companies' campaigns to portray smoking as a healthful, sophisticated activity. However, as medical evidence about smoking's harm accumulated in the 1960s, the public slowly, but surely, began to understand the true issues involved, and the number and percentage of smokers began declining. Moreover, scientific knowledge, now more effectively disseminated by the mass media of television and radio, created new possibilities for learning, and the public, in being brought into the mass communication age, has learned a new way of learning.

Similarly, changing the ingrained habits of excess violence in professional sports is likely to take some time and education, as spectators, administrators, and players learn new approaches to their sport. But there is certainly reason to hope that change is possible. In hockey, for instance, due to the rule changes in the early 1990s, fighting has substantially abated. Moreover, hockey fans are no longer as apt to go to games to revel in the nightly blood baths that used to dominate the sport. True, there are still fights, but the bench-clearing brawls that were common several years ago are now rare, for long suspensions for players and coaches have taken the edge off most players' ardor for beyond the rules excesses.

The training that the martial arts, Aikido and T'ai Chi Ch'uan particularly, can provide for professional athletes in team sports can be a vital part of controlling violence in that it can inculcate a new way to learn. As Linden maintains, "the real goal of Aikido practice is to learn how to learn. The goal is to find out how to use the training as a situation in which to create and direct philosophical change."27

Linden, and other teachers and commentators on the martial arts, focus on the concept of "being centered" as the main difference in terms of how conventional sports skills are taught and how martial arts are taught. That is, "being centered" has a physical, a psychological, and a philosophical orientation.

It manifests in the body as a firm, supple, balanced, and open body organization. It manifests in movement as freedom to move evenly, smoothly, and powerfully in all directions. It manifests psychologically as a calm, alert, fluid, and focused state of mind. And it manifests philosophically as a spirit of nonattachment, an ability to accept life as it is while at the same time working to change it to meet your wishes . . . being centered is at once a type of posture, a way of moving, a way of feeling, and a way of thinking.[28]

While learning how to learn is not exclusively an Eastern concept, the ways in which the martial arts have applied their concepts of learning in athletic training are deeply connected to the overall way in which they construct their ideas of reality. That is, learning how to learn has only partly to do with techniques and with practice; in a broader sense it has to do with a sort of spiritual connectedness to oneself that is not easily explainable in purely Western scientific-rationalist terms. In this regard, such commentators on applying the Zen tradition to Western sports training as Herrigal (*Zen in the Art of Archery*) and Gallwey (*The Inner Game of Tennis*) have been criticized for avoiding the full implications of the level of expertise of Zen Bones. Robert Sparks, among others, in his essay, "Mystical and material embodiment: A comparative analysis," complains that these books cannot explain the Zen master's skill, for the traditional Western way on which they largely rely for "Zen skill is a spiritual one and mystical expression cannot be understood in terms of material of physical embodiment."[29] Scott Watson, in his essay "Is there more to practice than the pursuit of perfection," echoes many of Sparks' points, and he underscores the need to incorporate elements of Eastern philosophy into Western sport training. Third, Chic Johnson's essay, "Toward a revisionist philosophy of coaching, "offers a look at an alternative that embodies aspects of Eastern and Western thought. A look at these three essays will further elucidate what it means to "learn how to learn" in Zen and martial arts terms.

Watson begins his argument by asserting that people are rarely fully aware of their own ontological commitments, that is, their commitment to the relationships between people. In other words, the way someone involved in sport practices that sport invariably reflects their ontological commitment, whether or not the person is consciously aware of the nature of his or her commitment. In order to explicate his position on the unity of ontology and methodology, Watson uses Eugen Herrigal's 1953 book (reprinted in 1971), *Zen and the Art of Archery*, in contrast to Gallwey's 1974 book, *The Inner Game of Tennis*.

Put simply, while Herrigal understands that the way one practices projects one's underlying spiritual commitments, Gallwey simply abstracts the techniques of Zen in order to increase one's skill level. As Watson sees Herrigal's way of learning, it reflects a spiritual level of being:

> The foremost objective of Herrigal's practice was to detach himself from all care and concern, even from the concern with hitting the target or shooting correctly. Herrigal was instructed to practice technique . . . in order to achieve what might be called the 'everyday mind,' which is without reflection, deliberation, or conceptualization. Such practice, through methodological immersion in oneself or immersion in the form or technique of what one is doing leads to self-detachment...[As] discussed by Herrigal, the methodology of the art of archery . . . involves virtually a single concern to the point that the students are admonished at times not to practice 'anything except self-detached immersion.'[30]

Robert Sparks, in his essay, "Mystical and material embodiment: A comparative analysis," makes a strong case that the traditional rationalist-scientific training and thinking that dominates sport and physical education needs to be revised in light of the leading edge of thinking in such fields as physics. His thesis is that there is misunderstanding inherent "in all attempts . . . to explain mystical expression in terms of material or physical embodiment."[31]

In making his case, Sparks focuses on David Bohm and Karl Pribham's vision of a "holographic paradigm" that has already begun to replace the inflexible view of physical reality that has come to us as a result of taking Cartesian dualism to its extreme. The "holographic paradigm" is based on the peculiarities of the hologram, as Sparks explains:

> A hologram is a record made on a photographic plate when light from a laser is split by a mirror and allowed to bounce off a subject, then merge back with its own beam at the surface of a plate. The resultant interference pattern gets recorded and can subsequently be used to create a three-dimensional image in space by reversing the pro-cedure . . . The image recorded, unlike a lens-focused image in a camera, is stored in its entirety throughout the hologram. Thus, like the mystical notion of interpenetration, the holographic image is timelessly interspersed across its film surface . . . The result is such that if you break off one small piece of the hologram, you still have the entire image that was illuminated recorded on that piece.[32]

Some of the same implications of the holographic paradigm were explored by several scientists and philosophers in an important 1982 collection of essays and interviews, *The Holographic Paradigm and Other Paradoxes*, edited by the biochemist and writer, Ken Wilber. One of the interviews, conducted by Renee Weber with the renowned theoretical physicist, David Bohm, gives a sense of what the new paradigm—a unity of spirituality, science, and psychology—looks like. Bohm and Karl Pribham, a neuroscientist, have developed a new model which diverges greatly from the Cartesian model upon which much of modern thinking has been based. Bohm focuses on the consciousness of humankind as being one and not truly divisible, a lesson he took from his knowledge of quantum mechanics and theoretical physics. Bohm termed his holographic paradigm as an "enfolding-infolding universe," explaining the phenomenon in the following way:

> The ordinary description of physics is the Cartesian order in which we take a Cartesian grid and we say all points are entirely outside of each other and have a contiguous relation. You can then make a smooth curve for example, but if we enfolded that smooth curve we would get a whole with everything interpenetrating, and yet it would unfold into a smooth curve. Another smooth curve could be folded up. The result would look the same, very nearly, and yet the two would be different. So there would be a set of distinctions that we make which are different from those that we make in the ordinary Cartesian order; namely, that there are all these enfolded orders which are different and yet don't look different from the gross view, from the ordinary view.[33]

Further, in an essay in Wilber's book elaborating upon Bohm's theories, Ken Dychtwald outlines several aspects of this new paradigm:

1. There is actually no such thing as pure energy or pure matter. Every aspect of the universe seems neither to be a thing or no-thing, but rather exists as a kind of vibrational or energetic expression. . . .
2. Every aspect of the universe is itself a whole, a full being, a comprehensive system in its own right, containing within it a complete store of information about itself. . . .
3. Every aspect of the universe seems to be part of some larger whole, grander being, and more comprehensive system....

4. Since each aspect of the universe expresses itself vibrationally, and all vibrational expressions intermingle within the master hologram(s), every aspect of the universe contains knowledge of the whole(s) within which it exists. . . .
5. Within the holographic paradigm, time does not exist as a ticking away of moments forever traveling linearly from 'now' to 'just then.' Instead, time might very well exist multidimensionally moving in many directions simultaneously.[34]

One way of looking at the process of developing a mind/body unity in an athlete has to do with the concept of "resonance." As Michael Talbot notes in his 1991 volume, *The Holographic Universe*, a psychologist, Robert M. Anderson, Jr., likens our ability to perceive the unity of various aspects of reality to a vibrating tuning fork:

We are only able to tap into information in the implicate order that is directly relevant to our memories. Anderson calls this selective process personal resonance and likens it to the fact that a vibrating tuning fork will resonate with (or set up a vibration in) another tuning fork only if the second tuning fork possesses a similar structure, shape, and size.[35]

Looked at in this way, when an athlete concentrates on developing a unity between himself and his opponent in order to compete, he or she is actually setting up a resonance with the competitor. In attaining this resonance, the athlete obtains access to his/her opponent's responsive processes within the context of a master holographic reality wherein each part contains the whole.

Indeed, had the original practitioners of aikido and T'ai Chi had access to the holographic theory of reality, they likely would have found it quite compatible with the ways in which they advocate thinking about one's opponents. Certainly, Ming's "fields of consciousness" echoes Anderson's "resonance" principle in that the central concept of both involve aligning one's energy with that of one's opponent.

The Cartesian view of the world—that pieces of reality can be studied and analyzed with little or no reference to the context in which they are placed or the unity of the thing to all other things is eroding, even within the scientific community. In disciplines that are less tied to traditional scientific-rationalist thought, including sports training and physical education, this erosional process hopefully will continue at an even faster pace than in the past decades, partly due to the influence of such activities as Aikido and T'ai Chi Ch'uan. As Sparks notes, "scientific explanations of mysticism inherently reduce the internal to the external,"[36] and the processes of physical training simply can not be reduced to empirical-analytical knowledge.

Shi Ming and the nature of consciousness

In Bill Moyer's highly acclaimed 1993 PBS television series, *Healing and the Mind*, Shi Ming, a master of Chinese martial arts, gave a remarkable demonstration of the inner power of his techniques and philosophy. In his book, *Mind Over Matter*, Ming offers a view of martial arts that includes their historical and philosophical underpinnings. Moreover, Ming explores in some depth the holistic interactions of the martial arts and Chinese culture, emphasizing the fact that the higher martial arts have "been sublimated from fighting into a way of seeking the Tao," that is, Truth. This Truth that the Tao contains is neither the "scientific" proof of Western culture, nor is it related to a non-physical reality that is separate from physical creation. Rather, the Tao is the undivided unity of all physical and non-physical creation, and it thus represents a transcendence of duality.

As with other forms of martial arts, Chinese higher martial arts rely on exercises to control one's breath as essential to developing proper control of one's energies:

> The basic principle of the training, that inside and outside join, enables people to gradually attain intercourse and merging of the totality of body and mind. The special training of consciousness and the respiratory system, gradually advancing, effectively regulates every system of the mechanical body as well as the technical capacities of the whole being; it regulates the entire nervous system and endocrine system, and at the same time gradually leads to a higher level of harmony and integration of the self with the external world (including both nature and society).[37]

One important distinction that Ming draws between Western ideas and Eastern ones concerns the term "refinement of consciousness." That is, most Westerners would automatically assign "consciousness" to the domain of psychology, and in the context of sport, to the psychology of athletics. However, Ming (and other martial artists) use this expression quite differently, to refer to "a high level of conscious perception of the biological processes of the human body in movement, especially biodynamics."[38]

Within the context of martial arts, then, "consciousness has a narrow meaning and a broad meaning," the narrow one referring to the " supranormal biodynamic psychology" advocated by Gallwey and others. However, the broader meaning of consciousness includes "enhanced conscious perception of the capacities of the human body and mind."[39] Part of this enhanced perception involves focusing internal energy so that it is projected effectively outside the body.

It is certain that many of the exceptionally gifted athletes who achieve the excellence of professionals understand that energy can be most effectively projected, both in sports contests and in other endeavors, when intent amplifies their skills through awareness of their individual biofeedback system and through imaginative visualization of their intended result. Gallwey, among others, repeatedly emphasizes techniques to help with biofeedback and visualization. In Ming's view, however, the notion of projecting one's energy takes on another level of meaning, for projected energy creates what he calls "a field of consciousness and energy." That is, in a cooperative interaction of consciousness, thought, and intent, the martial artist can "create at will a formless consciousness field that can be deliberately controlled." As Ming explains it, this concept also includes "a corresponding dynamic effect, which could be called a field effect":

> When a human body that has been made into a conductor of power transmits (or releases) that power into a space, this power is no longer subject to the limitations of the structure of the conductor. Furthermore . . . it departs from the medium of a solid body and an electric body (i.e., the human body), thus coming under the direct control of conscious thought.

> When this power reaches open space, then it is "energy." It could also be called a field of consciousness and energy . . . or the energy of consciousness. This can be concentrated and dispersed . . . it can take on any mode of movement and spatial dimension desired. Furthermore, in the context of elevating one's own powers of response to the environment . . . it activates a field effect that has practical usefulness.[40]

It is, of course, well beyond the scope of this book to offer objective scientific proof that human beings are capable of creating such an externalized "field of consciousness," partly because no such "objective" proof can exist within the context of the current Western mind/body split. From Ming's Chinese point of view, "the reason that modern science finds it extremely difficult to study this phenomenon . . . is that present day techniques of brain science have not yet developed to a level where they can measure the various levels of interaction among thought, intent, consciousness, and vitality-energy-spirit."[41]

In terms of this discussion of controlling violence in professional sports, the specific techniques for controlling energy that Ming advocates can certainly help the athlete reach a calmer center. That is, understanding of the philosophy and mechanics of how energy is effectively projected toward a goal and/or toward a fellow competitor can offer the athlete a way to enhance his skills that goes beyond what can be accomplished through training only the body, or even training both the mind and the body.

Moreover, the concept of "group mind," as it is reflected in the idea of team sports may also be useful in athletic training. That is, if the team can operate as a unified whole, coming into resonance with each other, they will be better able to anticipate their teammates' moves and intentions. In fact, it seems likely that many players can feel a sense of resonance with teammates. For instance, the best point guards in professional basketball may make the best use of such resonance, and this is reflected in their seemingly miraculous ability to anticipate where to throw a pass. No doubt, much of their basketball acumen stems from countless hours of practice and concentration, but for the best of them, even talent, practice, and concentration cannot explain the full range of their skills.

Thus, learning how to learn involves reconstructing our ideas about reality to include the sort of world view that is suggested by Uyeshiba, Ming, Linden, Sparks, Bohm, Pribham, Talbot, Anderson, and others. How to put such an updated model, one that incorporates aspects of Eastern thinking, into practice as a coach or physical education teacher is the focus of Chic Johnson's intriguing article, "Toward a revisionist philosophy of coaching," as well as the chapter "Zen and Yoga in Sport" in Spencer Wertz's book, *Talking a Good Game*. The next section explores Wertz's and Johnson's approach, as well as others, in an effort to suggest ways that athletic training can include an expanded, and more powerful, vision of reality.

A Unitary Approach to Training and Coaching

The application of Eastern martial arts training techniques to professional football, basketball, or baseball may seem to be a stretch to many coaches and players who have been inculcated in an exclusively Western approach to learning and playing sports. However, it is my contention that this resistance to Eastern methods of thinking has largely to do with ignorance of their ultimate effectiveness. Indeed, there is a good deal of anecdotal information that suggests that many of the best professional athletes reach a meditative consciousness on the field of play that is the equivalent of the state of mind advocated by Uyeshiba and others in the practice of Aikido and T'ai Chi Ch'uan.

As long ago as 1975, the pseudonymous Adam Smith, writing in *Psychology Today*, insisted that "pros in football, diving, basketball, golf, and tennis now sound like Zen masters," elaborating on his point by quoting John Brodie, the former San Francisco Forty-niners' quarterback:

> Sometimes in the heat of a game a player's perception and coordination improve dramatically. At times, I experience a kind of clarity that I've never seen described in any football story; sometimes time seems to slow way down, as if I have all the time in the world to watch the receivers run their patterns, and yet I know the defensive line is coming at me just as fast as ever, and yet the whole thing sounds like a movie or a dance in slow motion. It's beautiful.[42]

Nor is football the only sport wherein players achieve this sort of state of mind. Bill Bradley, former United States Senator from New Jersey, but previously a professional basketball player for the New York Knicks, insisted that "the secret of shooting is concentration," and he prepared for games in a meditative way. As quoted in Wertz, Bradley's attitude echoes the discipline of the martial arts:

> During the afternoon, when any other player in his situation would probably have been watching television, shooting pool, or playing ping-pong or poker—anything to divert the mind—Bradley sat alone and concentrated on the coming game, on the components of his own play, and on the importance to him and his team of what would occur.[43]

The chapter "Zen and Yoga in Sport" in *Talking a Good Game: Inquiries into the Principles of Sport* by Spencer K. Wertz offers an intriguing suggestion as to how the sort of mind set of a John Brodie or Bill Bradley can be at least partially trained into less meditatively inclined athletes. Drawing on Gallwey's approach to tennis and on Deshimaru's approach to martial arts, Wertz maintains that the forms of the martial arts are quite like the "various moves and shots in basketball":

> The reverse pivot, the rocker step, going back door, finger roll, layups, the jump shot, hook shot, foul shot, and so on, have the same sort of exercises, practices, rituals, and mimes that are embedded in the martial arts—the step forward and strike with shoulder, mirror trails elbow, white crane spreads wings, brush knee and push, snake creeps down, golden cock on one leg, and so forth. The preparation skills and practice make these moves second nature to the participants.[44]

Wertz further suggests that "this model is easily adapted to other realms of human movement," in what he calls the "Sports Episode (SE)," a series of six movements that can be trained in individuals: "(1) reaction, (2) preparation, (3) movement toward opponent, (4) opponent contact, (5) recovery, and (6) positioning for the next move or form."[45] Just as in the martial arts, each move must initially be practiced separately, but the aim is that the moves eventually are internalized to the extent that Bill Bradley was able to internalize shooting the basketball: "'When you have played basketball for a while, you don't need to look at the basket when you are in close like this,' he said, throwing it over his shoulder . . . right through the hoop."[46] As Wertz states, "Bradley's locational sense is comparable to the state of awareness of one's environment in Zen."[47]

Chic Johnson makes a much more concerted effort at developing a philosophy of coaching that dissolves the apparent contradictions between Eastern and Western approaches to sport. Johnson cites Alan Watts, Gallwey and Leonard as authorities on developing and maintaining the proper mind set toward the enterprise of sport, a mind set which emphasizes the Zen concept of "no-mind," as opposed to conventional ways of concentration. Watts, quoting the eighth century Zen master, Shen-hui, describes this "no-mind" wisdom as opposed to concentration. Indeed, "all cultivation of concentration is wrong-minded from the start," Shen-hui asserts. For how, by cultivating concentration, could one obtain concentration?"[48]

One way of conceptualizing this state of "no mind," as suggested earlier, involves the idea of resonance. Rather than trying to think out how an opponent is going to react to a particular strategy, the competitor cultivating "no mind" seeks to set up a resonance that stems from the master holographic reality in which competitors share.

Further, Johnson notes that athletes today are not as prone to accepting authority figures, and hence training, as they were in the past. The socio-cultural environment has made the command-and-control oriented coaching style more than a little obsolete, particularly among athletes that have been raised in an urban setting. Thus, "the insightful and perceptive contemporary coaches are becoming cognizant of the necessity to challenge the athlete mentally and psychologically."[49]

There are several central attributes that such a coach can help the athlete cultivate, as Johnson outlines them:

Harmony of mind, body, and spirit, and an ability to unite the internal with the external. . . .

A deeply marked sense of responsibility for one's life and the desire to design alternative futures. Knowing what is in one's best interests involves quieting the mind while gently assessing the here and now. The most valuable experiences of our lives are those in which we are called upon to take a risk, to act on a decision, to make a choice.

Willingness to reevaluate belief systems and traditions, to choose intuitively, not only rationally. Being open to new systems and alternate values requires an ability to continually 'let go' and select new forms. The only thing that we can speak of with any degree of certainty is that things will change.

A compelling drive to grow, to discover, to evolve in contrast to conquering, controlling, and coercing. The difference between growing and conquering lies primarily in the quality and feeling of the action.[50]

The sort of coach who can focus on the underlying values of sport for the individual, rather than merely on the idea that "winning is everything," will ultimately be more successful with many of the most physically gifted athletes, for maintaining a gifted athlete's motivation is increasingly important. The old style control and command coach who focuses exclusively or principally on developing skills and little on the mental aspects of sport preparation can not hope to properly motivate his athletes, and this is certainly a socio-cultural trend that will continue for the foreseeable future. Of course, physical practice will never be an outmoded form of athletic preparation, and coaches must still pay attention to this part of their job.

However, the element of mental preparation can certainly help alleviate the problems of beyond the rules violence by refocusing the athlete's values toward improving his performance rather than towards conquering his opponent. In the long run, perhaps in a generation, athletes can be taught that they can perform better, more effectively, by concentrating on self-improvement in the manner suggested by Uyeshiba's philosophy of Aikido. Certainly, in order to accomplish this change in attitude, coaches will have to increasingly incorporate aspects of mental and psychological training in their repertoire.

But how far can we expect Western-trained coaches to use Eastern mental and psychological conditioning methods in their approaches? The answer, according to Johnson, may lie within the realm of the developing scientific field of *anthropomaximology*: the study of the upper limits of human capability. That is, if coaches can be convinced through science that Eastern approaches to maximizing performance actually work, they may be increasingly more willing to incorporate them in their coaching behavior. As Johnson elaborates:

The techniques of anthropomaximology include psychic self-regulation (PSR), deep relaxation, mental imagery, and mental rehearsal. PSR theory has a neurophysiological base. When a person is in a state of profound relaxation, the brain and central nervous system cannot distinguish between a deeply imprinted image and the physical event. For example, if an athlete preparing for a particular feat can achieve a sufficient depth of relaxation and clarity of image and can imagine him or herself successfully completing the feat, the brain and central nervous system imprint the event as though the body has actually experienced it with the concomitant changes even in pulse and blood pressure. The achievement of the actual feat can then be accomplished with an ease and effortlessness generally unmatched by physical training alone.[51]

Thus, part of the answer of how to unite Eastern and Western approaches may be in studying the ultimate scientific validity of the mind set that the martial arts strives to teach. This can be done partly through biofeedback techniques which have been developed in the past two decades, since Elmer and Alyce Green, pioneers in the field, presciently wrote in the mid-1970s that "it is necessary to give to mind a role in nature that has heretofore not been acceptable in modern science."

*****

Some scientists do not like this, but there is no way to avoid it. The evidence is overwhelming and can no longer be ignored. In the twenty-first century it will be taken for granted by every schoolchild that mind and matter, both inside and outside the skin, have something in common . . . A significant factor [in twenty-first century science] will be 'self-awareness.'[52]

Training athletes in biofeedback techniques has become commonplace since the Greens wrote *Beyond Biofeedback*, but far more use can be made of these techniques in terms of demonstrating to coaches and athletes that the mind can control many aspects of the body's responses, particularly that the relaxation techniques advocated by martial artists such as Ron Sieh work quite well. Part of the difficulty is in terminology, as many coaches and athletes think of "relaxation" as somehow tied to a lack of discipline. However, as Sieh notes, in T'ai Chi, "what we use to direct our movement is not helped by physical (or mental) contraction, tension."[53]

Sieh's technique of relaxation is consonant with many other martial artists' techniques, and it is deceptively simple in that the first essential step is the decision to relax: "we have to know if 'relaxed' is truly what we want to be." Of course, making a conscious decision to relax does not, in and of itself, relax a person; however, it is the most essential first step. Then, the process of relaxing involves a simple technique: when standing, the idea is to arrange oneself so as to "accommodate gravity rather than to struggle against it." This involves standing "into our feet with our bodies stacked upwards from the ground, the piece above resting atop the piece below."[54] Further, Sieh maintains that he starts "by actually tensing my legs, tightening them up, then slowly softening them, doing this several times."[55]

Training Morally Acceptable Societal Attitudes

Beyond the techniques of martial arts and the philosophy behind Eastern approaches to the body/mind dichotomy lie a number of troublesome questions. How can we encourage young people to alter their attitudes towards violence both on and off the playing field? Can morality be trained, especially given the terrible socio-economic problems that accompany the grinding poverty that many professional athletes have struggled mightily to escape? Is altering the training methods, rules, and enforcement processes enough to make more than a brief splash in an ocean of unnecessary violence?

The answer to these questions is partly that, except in cases of natural or man-made disasters, all deep societal changes in philosophic outlook are gradual, and a focused effort to retrain our cultural morality is bound to have an impact, even if that impact is not immediately evident. Furthermore, to maintain that people's behavior cannot be altered ignores the many ways in which our culture's behavior has already been changed by the concerted efforts of people, government, and organizations, such as with the public's smoking and seat belt wearing habits.

Regardless of the fact that a certain amount of violence is endemic to the professional sports we watch, it is incumbent on us as a society to insist that professional sports offer us a palatable form of entertainment, one that reflects the values that our culture needs as well as the values that we already have acquired. If the mind/body split that has gripped Western thought, particularly since Descartes, is not tempered by including an infusion of philosophic alloys in its metal, our culture will become increasingly brittle, and our sports will continue to view beyond the rules violence as necessary.

The martial arts offer an alternative way of thinking about the opponent and oneself, an importantly different way of understanding the ultimate unity of body and mind, for when these two human aspects work as a unity, improved performance can be realized by athletes at all levels of skill. As Ming insists:

> . . . martial arts develop dynamic thought in people through refinement of consciousness, thence to develop higher apperception. In the course of this process, it is necessary to attain unification of body and mind, a level of coordination with the natural laws of the universe. This coordination, and only this coordination, makes it possible to develop the highest human character, the highest morality, and the highest spiritual state. Only with this spiritual state is it possible to dissolve the boundaries and contradictions between public and private realms. And only with this spiritual state is it possible to benefit humankind in a manner that is truly complete and effective.[56]

In other words, if the symptom is violence within our cultural institutions, including professional sports, the disease is our insistence that mind and body can be viewed as ultimately separate.

Notes

1. Paul Reps, p. 92.
2. Shi Ming, p. 3.
3. R. Scott Kretchmer, "Ethics and Sport." *Journal of the Philosophy of Sport*, X, 1983, p. 22.
4. Of course, progress in such areas as reducing smoking does not happen unabated. At the same time the Surgeon General's office insists on warning labels and engages in educational efforts to cut smoking's health toll, the Department of Agriculture offers subsidies to tobacco farmers.
5. Montagu, p. 6.
6. John D. Curtis, *The Mindset for Winning* (LaCrosse, WI: Coulee Press, 1991), p. 1.
7. Hanna, p. 179.
8. Roger Sperry, "Some Effects of Disconnecting the Cerebral Hemispheres." *Science*, 217, September 24, 1982, p. 1226.
9. Such eminent physicists as Wolfgang Pauli, the 1945 Nobel laureate, long ago recognized the limitations of rationalist thought when it came to physics.
10. John Stevens and Shirata Rinjiro. *Aikido: The Way of Harmony*. Boston: Shambhala, 1984, pp. 3-4.
11. Stevens, p. 7.
12. Stevens, p. 7.
13. Stevens, p. 18.
14. Stevens, p. 25.
15. George Leonard, *The Ultimate Athlete*, p. 231.
16. Olson and Comfort, p. 102.
17. Leonard, p. 231.
18. Leonard, p. 234.
19. Riley, p. 176.
20. Olson and Comfort, p. 102.
21. Gregory D. Olson and Norman D. Comfort, III, p. 103.
22. Carl Gustav Jung (1875-1961), the Swiss psychoanalyst and metaphysician, used the term "synchronicity" to refer to events that happen with too much inner consistency to be attributed to coincidence and yet are not connected through normal cause and effect mechanisms.
23. Tem Horwitz, Susan Kimmelman, and H.H. Lui. *T'ai Chi Ch'uan: The Technique of Power*. Chicago: Chicago Review Press, 1976, p. 59.
24. Olson and Comfort, p. 103.
25. Leonard, pp. 230-231.
26. Riley, p. 53.
27. Paul Linden. "The art of aikido: Philosophical education in movement." *In Mind and Body: East Meets West*, Seymour Kleinman, ed. Champaign, IL: Human Kinetics, 1986, p. 110.

28. Linden, p. 110.
29. Seymour Kleinman, p. 129.
30. Scott B. Watson. "Is there more to practice than the pursuit of perfrction?" In *Mind and Body: East Meets West*, Seymour Kleinman, ed. Champaign, IL: Human Kinetics Publishers, 1986, pp. 133-134.
31. Robert Sparks. "Mystical and Material Embodiment: A Comparative Analysis." In *Mind and Body: East Meets West*. Champaign, IL: Human Kinetics Publishers, 1986, p. 137.
32. Sparks, p. 141.
33. David Bohm and Renee Weber. "The Enfolding-Unfolding Universe: A Conversation with David Bohm." In *The Holographic Paradigm and Other Paradoxes*, Ken Wilber, ed. Boulder, CO: Shambhala Publications, 1982, p. 47.
34. Ken Dychtwald. "Commentaries on the Holcgraphic Theory: Reflections on the Holographic Paradigm." In *The Holographic Paradigm and Other Paradoxes*, Ken Wilber, ed. Boulder, CO: Shambhala Publications, 1982, pp. 109-112.
35. Talbot, p. 61.
36. Sparks, p. 147.
37. Shi Ming, p. xvii.
38. Ming, p. 49.
39. Ming, pp. 49-50.
40. Ming, p. 58.
41. Ming, p. 58.
42. Adam Smith (pseudonym). "Sport Is a Western Yoga." *Psychology Today*, IX (October 1975), pp. 48-50.
43. Wertz, p. 135.
44. Wertz, p. 136.
45. Wertz, p. 136.
46. Wertz, p. 135.
47. Wertz, p. 140.
48. Alan Watts. *The Way of Zen*. New York: Pantheon, 1957, p. 96.
49. Chic Johnson. "Toward a revisionist philosophy coaching." In *Mind and Body: East Meets West*, Seymour Kleinman, ed. Champaign, IL: Human Kinetics Publishers, 1986, p. 153.
50. Johnson, p. 153.
51. Johnson, pp. 154-155.
52. Elmer Green and Alyce Green. *Beyond Biofeedback*. New York: Delacorte Press, 1977, pp. 1-2.
53. Sieh, p. 29.
54. Ibid., p. 29.
55. Ibid., p. 30.
56. Ming, p. 102.

Chapter 6

ಸಂಚ

A Critique of Violence
in Professional Sports

Introduction

There will always be a degree of beyond the rules violence in professional sports, for athletes must rely on strong emotions to bring them to their peak performances, and sometimes emotions flow beyond the individual's immediate control, even for most of those athletes who have some training in setting up energetic resonance with the opponent. Certainly, too, some of our sports—football and hockey, particularly—are by their nature violent, whatever rules are adopted to minimize beyond the rules violence. Nevertheless, violence that does serious injury to another must be actively discouraged, and those athletes who repeatedly rely on beyond the rules violence must be controlled or evicted from their sports. Moreover, they must be imprisoned for serious enough breaches of our laws, just as individuals in other occupations would be jailed for intentionally causing harm to others.

If we can, as a culture, alter the trend toward excessive violence in professional sports, it will be through training the young athlete that rules must be adhered to if he wishes to continue playing, and eventually

making a living at, a game that has been elevated to high pop culture
entertainment status by virtue of huge stadiums, enormously increased
television coverage, and rampant commercialism. If brawls are common,
if serious injuries frequently are the result of win-at-all-costs brutality,
and if the playing field or court has radically different limits for beyond-
the-laws violent behavior than is true elsewhere in society, it will be at
least substantially because young athletes see that the way to succeed is
to brawl and intimidate when skill and talent are not sufficient to win the
game, the ten million dollar contract, and the mega-million dollar
endorsement deals.

   In re-training our young athletes and in re-programming our ethical
values as regards professional sports, we can make use of some of the
principles of Eastern approaches to the mind/body link. Indeed, in many
sports, from tennis to golf to professional basketball, sports educators
are increasingly making use of training techniques grafted from pioneers
such as Timothy Gallwey.

   There are values to using an inward-directed approach for the athlete
or for the ordinary person that go well beyond the limits of the game,
values that the game can help teach. For, as Gallwey insisted more than
twenty years ago:

> Not only can these inner skills have a remarkable effect on one's
> forehand, backhand, serve, and volley (the outer game of tennis), but
> they are valuable in themselves and have broad applicability to other
> aspects of life. When a player learns to recognize, for instance, that
> learning to concentrate may be more valuable to him than a backhand,
> he shifts from being primarily a player of the outer game to being a
> player of the Inner Game. Then, instead of learning concentration to
> improve his tennis, he practices tennis to improve his concentration. . . .
> Competition then becomes an interesting device in which each player,
> by making his maximum effort to win, gives the other the opportunity
> he desires to reach new levels. . . .[1]

   In the following pages, I review the major findings of my research
into controlling violence in professional sports in America, taking each
of this book's three major hypotheses[2] and discussing them individually
before offering a general summation. Because of the breadth of the
influence of professional sports in America, it is not possible to touch on
all of the subtle ways our culture and our youth are affected by sport
violence; however, in elucidating the major outlines of a treatment for

this societal disease, it is hoped that other cultural surgeons, ones with particular expertise in individual sports, will be able to apply the principles outlined here to reduce the level of violence in their sport.

The Three Hypotheses

American Team Sports Are Too Violent

My first hypothesis was that American sport, particularly at the professional, major team sport level, is unacceptably violent, in terms of the ethical values such violence teaches younger sport participants.

If the history of professional sports teaches us nothing else, it should be clear that the connection between money and willingness to use beyond the rules violence is basic. That is, when a great deal of money is at stake, athletes will tend to do precisely as most other people will do: anything they think they can get away with in pursuit of their goal. If excessive, on-the-field violence is their ticket out of poverty, many athletes will adopt a frame of reference that allows them to justify their actions. Since the days of the original Olympic Games, concepts of "fair play" have often taken a lower priority than winning, for professional athletes' careers are frequently "short, brutish, and nasty," to steal a line from the poet, Alexander Pope.

Moreover, the transformation of athletes into people who are willing to bend the rules through the use of violence to gain an edge begins early in the gifted athlete's career. As Jack Tatum, a one-time Oakland Raider linebacker, known as "the Assassin," described the process of desensitization:

> When I first started playing, if I would hit a guy hard and he wouldn't get up, it would bother me. [But] when I was a sophomore in high school, first game, I knocked out two quarterbacks, and people loved it. The coach loved it. The more you play, the more you realize that it is just part of the game-somebody's gonna get hurt. It could be you, it could be him—most of the time it's better if it's him.[3]

As many football fans may remember, in 1978, it was Tatum whose vicious hit broke Darryl Stingley's neck, leaving him a permanent paraplegic. While his hit was technically "legal," that is, it was within the rules of the game, Tatum's attitude that he would get away with whatever level of violence he could, an attitude inculcated from his earliest athletic experiences, is indicative of a societally unacceptable attitude toward violence.

Indeed, many people argue that it is useless to blame athletes for such injuries as Stingley's, for our culture revels in violence in ways that few others around the world do. As I discuss in the next section, this sort of attitude is only partially valid, for a democracy such as ours is premised on ideas of individual responsibility. That is, the individual must be held accountable for his or her actions, especially when the laws of the land are clearly violated by an act of violence performed in front of tens of thousands or, in the case of an event like the Super Bowl, many millions of fans.

There is certainly an excess of violence in professional sport; indeed, there has always been an excess of violence in sports, particularly in ones that provided financial rewards. Fortunately, our culture does not sanction the sort of unrestrained violence that characterized the worst of the Roman gladiatorial games or even the early days of American college football. Moreover, the protective gear that the modern football and hockey players wear is certainly better than it was even twenty years ago, and medical techniques allow for recovery from some types of injuries that would have permanently disabled athletes even a decade ago. Doc Rivers, for instance, now a player on the San Antonio Spurs, ruptured his anterior cruciate ligament in a game in December of 1993. By November of 1994, he was back on the court, despite the fact that such an injury would have ended his career any time before the early 1980s when arthroscopic surgery techniques were perfected.

Nevertheless, as a culture, we need to discourage the sort of violence that encourages others to play sports with the idea that "winning is the only thing." Doc Rivers' injury was not the result of beyond the rules violence; it was the result of a simple misstep while playing basketball with the intensity necessary to compete at the highest level. The injuries that players normally incur, and recover from, are part of the price of pushing one's body and spirit to their limits. The same injuries, when the result of beyond the rules violence, create even graver injuries to our country's collective psyche that are not so easy to expunge. Just as researchers are coming to the belated conclusion that so much violence on children's television contributes to the overall incidence of violence among children, so must beyond the rules violence on televised sports contribute to the next generation's acceptance of ever higher levels of unnecessary violence on the field, court, or rink.

Again, it is worth considering the holographic paradigm of reality, particularly the concept of resonance, in dealing with the societal effects of violence on both children and adults in our culture. Whether we like it or not, we all implicitly participate in our culture's group reality, its collective psyche, and players, coaches, fans, advertisers, and owners all have a responsibility to one another to recognize the effects of their thoughts and behaviors on one another. Although this cannot as yet be objectively proven, as the resonance of all of these groups comes more into their conscious intentions, it is likely that the level of beyond the rules violence will decrease considerably.

Strengthening Administrative and Legal Remedies

My second hypothesis is that administrative remedies to on the field, court, or rink violence must be strengthened, and some of the most recent rules changes suggest more effective means by which excessive violence in professional sports can be curtailed.

A large part of the problem concerning administrative remedies involves the sports' willingness to pre-emptively take strong measures to control their own sports. It seems that many administrators think like many of the athletes: whatever makes money for the individual and the team is acceptable. They will put up with a violent player if the fans keep coming into the stadium and the television revenues keep flowing. Ethical issues are simply not part of their equation, that is until fans insist that the administrators deal with what those fans perceive to be an excess of violence.

The administrative attitude toward excessive violence in professional sports also is made evident by their secrecy concerning the exact wording of their rules and regulations. When this researcher attempted to acquire copies of the official rules and regulations from the four major professional sports (baseball, basketball, football, hockey), none of the league offices were cooperative. Indeed, they are quite suspicious of anyone who is writing about violence in sports, for they perceive such articles to be potentially harmful to their bottom line. And, of course, there have been a large number of critical articles about professional sports in recent years, and they are thus even less likely to cooperate with journalistic or academic writers who would potentially make their jobs harder by exposing them to more negative publicity. The recent labor disputes in baseball and hockey may have further hardened their resolve to minimize criticism, for the press did not spare the owners and the leagues any venom just because the players, too, were perceived by the public as being greedy. Changing this administrative attitude may prove to be every bit as difficult as changing the athletes' attitudes.

Regardless of the attitudes of sport administrators and athletes, it is up to society to police what happens on the field of play if events go beyond the legal limits. Leaving enforcement of all activities that occur within the context of professional sport to the teams and players is like leaving the fox and the cat in charge of the henhouse: they simply cannot be fully trusted to do a thorough job themselves, even if they occasionally go after each other as well as the chickens.

In this regard, society can take two important actions to force administrators to be more responsive to the needs to minimize excessive violence in their sports. First, the public can speak through extra-legal means: non-attendance of games, an insistence to sponsors that they tone down the violent content of sports-related advertisements, and a turning away from sports programs that give a great deal of play and replays to brawls, illegal hits, and brutish behavior. Second, there are a few changes in the way that professional sports enforces its rules that are at least worth a serious public debate.

In regards to the first remedy open to the public, letters to ESPN, the local newspaper, sports magazines, and league teams and offices do have a cumulative effect, for professional sports administrators increasingly have their fingers on the pulse of public opinion. As the enormous dip in public support of baseball following the long labor dispute that prematurely ended the 1994 season and delayed the start of the 1995 season indicates, there is not an unlimited reservoir of good will for sports when the public believes its interests have been violated. Furthermore, such withdrawal of support will get the club owners' attention, particularly during times when television contracts are being negotiated. Unless the networks think they can get sponsors to lay out their money to advertise on basebrawl, basketbrawl, or footbrawl nights, they won't keep feeding professional sports as many millions as they currently do.

Changes that come from public opinion are not uncommon. Indeed, the rules changes in the NBA for the 1994-95 season resulted in large part from the league's embarrassment at the level of violence displayed in the 1994 playoffs, climaxed by the New York Knicks-Indiana Pacers brouhaha on national television at the feet of David Stern, the league commissioner. And public opinion, helped immensely by a few sports journalists in *Sports Illustrated* and the major newspapers (principally the *New York Times*, the *Washington Post*, and *USA Today*), had a decisive effect on getting professional hockey to de-emphasize the importance of the brawl by strengthening the fighting rules to include lengthy suspensions for players and coaches.

Following are a number of changes that need to be considered in order to minimize the amount of beyond the rules violence in professional sports:

a. Limit or eliminate the consumption of alcohol

As the fuel of choice for fan-induced violence, there is no rival for alcohol. At the very least, sales of all alcoholic beverages should be forbidden in the last quarter or last two innings of a game in order to minimize fan-induced violence and to allow drivers a period of abstinence before getting into their cars and onto the streets and highways.

b. Turn down the noise and get rid of the mascots

The way in which some clubs try to manipulate the emotional level of the game, either through mascots (e.g., the Phillies Phanatic) or through noise (e.g., the race car noise played at Indiana Pacer's games during opponents' possessions) should be strictly controlled. When noise or mascots are used to build a level of frenzy that threatens to get out of control, it should be stopped.

c. Evict overly rowdy fans

While it may be a time-honored American cry to "kill the ump," and it may be accepted practice for some fans to heap sometimes personal abuse on individual players, this should no longer be tolerated. Put simply, we do not allow cries of "kill" against anyone outside of stadiums and arenas, and there is no reason to treat such threats less seriously within the context of professional sports. Moreover, certain kinds of verbal abuse are not allowed by law in other public venues, and no exception should be made for professional sports. After appropriate warnings, such chronic abusers should be banned from attendance.

d. Institute strong penalties for fighting

As previously mentioned, in hockey and basketball, the leagues have strengthened penalties for fighting. The most effective guarantee against brawls seems to have been instituted by the NHL when they started kicking the "third man on the ice" out of games in order to stop two-person fights from becoming outright brawls. In addition to such third man rules, stiffer fines and long suspensions without pay might curb fighting.

e. Control the marketing of violence

Controlling videos and commercials that market sports violence should be controlled, to the extent possible, by the leagues. While marketing income is now a substantial portion of players' and clubs' total income, the bottom line needs to make accommodations for the need to control the violence in sport. The glorifying of the explicitly violent aspects of sport in advertising, publicity, or concession sales must be avoided as part of this overall effort to eliminate beyond the rules violence.

Legal remedies to curb violence

Unfortunately, there are few straightforward legal remedies to controlling beyond the rules violence in professional sports. There are obvious problems with certain enforcement aspects; for instance, do we allow the police to arrest players on the field, inviting the possible wrath of thousands of beer-lubricated fans? However, regardless of the complications, legal issues must be seriously discussed.

a. Individual legal responsibilities

In brief, this book argues that a professional athlete should be held legally accountable for the intentional, beyond the rules injuries he inflicts on an opponent. This legal culpability should include the same financial and incarceration penalties as equivalent crimes in the non-sport world. While it may be difficult to determine such issues as criminal intent in the case of an on-the-field, rink, or court injury, intent is always a critical factor in determining the degree of guilt or innocence. In our form of democracy a judge or a jury is entrusted to make such legal determinations, and there is no clear rationale for exempting professional sports from our judicial system.

b. Legislation concerning sports violence

Although there have been sporadic attempts to pass a sports violence bill in Congress, it is unlikely that such a bill will be able to muster the votes for passage any time in the near future. Indeed, there are strong arguments for resisting the Federal government's additional intrusion into this arena, for state, local, and Federal laws already cover the crimes that can be committed during sports events.

The clubs' legal responsibilities

Clubs should be held financially responsible for injuries to other players, perhaps by assuming the cost of the injured player's lost services in the form of extensive fines or payments for the injured player's contract until the player returns to the sport. This would only pertain to cases where the infringement was clearly beyond the rules and the intent was to injure another player. But it would certainly discourage clubs from pushing players to use any means necessary to win. At some point "winning at all costs" has to be made so expensive, for both clubs and players, that a prohibitive cost can be found. Carlson's list of five penalties for the offending club, previously cited in Chapter Four, is an excellent place to start.

> The offending player's club should be made (1) to pay the salary of the injured player during his convalescence, (2) to pay his medical expenses, (3) to pay compensatory damages if he is unable to play in the future, (4) to pay fines for failing to control its own player's actions, and (5) to pay damages or relinquish draft choices to the injured player's club for the loss of his services.[4]

Moreover, banning chronic violators from the sport, perhaps even for life, might be a way of making penalties severe enough for an individual that he might temper his responses and actions. Basketball, in its institution of the " flagrant" foul rule, has taken a step in this direction. Hockey, in giving severe penalties to players who use their sticks to whack opponents heads, has also taken steps to outlawing fouls that might result in serious head injuries. Both basketball and hockey could go further, however, by unflinchingly stating that repeat violators may be permanently banned from the sport.

Re-uniting Body and Mind

My third hypothesis is that the values of Eastern, internally-directed ways of thinking about sport can help diminish the level of excessive violence by re-directing sport's natural aggression from an emphasis on punishing one's opponent to an emphasis on intensifying one's internal focus and improving one's athletic performance.

Changes at this level will not affect professional sport greatly for a time, as these changes require attitudinal changes in players that can only be gained from years of training. In one or two generations of athletes, perhaps as little as ten or fifteen years, educational efforts at the cultural level can bear fruit, just as the educational campaigns to wear seat belts and to cut down on alcohol consumption when driving have shown unmistakable signs of success.

The basic Western conception of a mind/body dichotomy has hindered progress in training athletes to adhere to an ethical code that prohibits violence intended to cause injury to an opponent, particularly when the offender knows that he has crossed the line between within the rules violence and beyond the rules violence. The unity that is the underpinning of the philosophies behind the Oriental martial arts, T'ai Chi Ch'uan and Aikido in particular, offers an alternative to our conventional, Cartesian view of a separate mind and body.

A number of principles are emphasized by these martial arts that could be usefully integrated into athletic training on all levels, from grade school through the professional ranks. Among the most important of these principles are the following three:

a. Practice compassion as a motivating force.

For George Leonard, this means that "winning is one element in the dance,"[5] that compassion actually allows a player to be more alert to the moves of his opponent, who is no longer viewed as an "enemy." The opponent should come to be regarded as an essential part of the process of testing oneself and one's progress.

b. Focus on spiritual connectedness with oneself.

Another result of our cultural acceptance of Cartesian rationalism has been to disconnect spirit with body. In this regard, Aikido and T'ai Chi can be of great benefit as part of athletic training processes. However, rather than advocate an approach that is connected to a particular religion, the most successful practitioners of this method meditate on methodology or technique as well as on a quite general sense of connectedness. In this regard, Karl Pribham and others who have been exploring the leading edge of metaphysics and physics, quantum mechanics and holographic theory, are demonstrating the existence of connections between all matter and energy that had previously not been elaborated fully.

c. Practice techniques of anthropomaximology

Anthropomaximology, the study of the upper limits of human capability, include psychic self-regulation, deep relaxation, mental imagery, and mental rehearsal. Biofeedback techniques can also be included in this list, as can a variety of relaxation techniques. Obviously, many coaches and athletes are already familiar with some of these techniques, and perhaps this is a tribute to how much certain "Eastern" values have already seeped into our collective consciousness.

d. Take the moral training of athletes more seriously

Morality can be trained, must be trained, if we want to assert societal control over beyond the rules violence. Martial arts, in developing dynamic thought in people through a process of refinement of consciousness, can greatly aid in the training of a more societally positive attitude concerning violence in general, and violence in professional sports. In offering a different way of understanding the opponent, oneself, and the unity of mind and body, the martial arts present a model that can be adapted to the needs of a variety of sports.

Notes

1. Timothy Gallwey, *The Inner Game of Tennis* (New York: Random House, 1974), p. 129.
2. See Introduction, pp. xii-xiii.
3. Michael A. Messner and Donald F. Sabo, p. 91.
4. Underwood, p. 96.
5. Leonard, *The Ultimate Athlete*, p. 231.

Bibliography

Abbal-Haqq, Ismat. *Violence in Sports*. Washington, D.C.: ERIC Clearinghouse on Teacher Education, 1989.

Abe, Shinobu. "Modern Sports and the Eastern Tradition of Physical Culture: Emphasizing Nishida's Theory of the Body." *Journal of the Philosophy of Sport*, v. XIV, 1987, pp. 43-47.

Abe, Shinobu. "Zen and Sport." *Journal of the Philosophy of Sport*, v. XIII, 1986, pp. 45-48.

Appenzeller, Herb. "Is the Law Ruining Sports?" *Update on Law-Related Education*, v. 7, n. 3, Fall 1983, pp. 43-44.

Araton, Harvey. "An Elbow, Followed by a Punch." *The New York Times*. April 11, 1993, p. 21.

Araton, Harvey. "NBA Dilemma: Boys Will Be Bad." *The New York Times*, April 11, 1993, p. 24.

Atyeo, Don. *Blood & Guts: Violence in Sports*. New York: Paddington Press, 1979.

Back, Allan and Daeshik Kim. "Toward a Western Philosophy of Eastern Martial Arts." *Journal of the Philosophy of Sport*, v. VI, 1979, pp. 19-28.

Beisser, Arnold M. *The Madness in Sports* (2nd ed.). Bowie, MD: The Charles Press: 1977.

Berkow, Ira. "Walking Away While He Still Can." *The New York Times*, Sunday, Oct. 3, 1993, section 8, pp. 1-2.

Betts, John Rickards. "The Technological Revolution and the Rise of Sport, 1850-1900." *Mississippi Valley Historical Review*, XL (September, 1953), pp. 231-256.

Bodley, Hal. "NL Boss Takes Hard Line on Outbreak of Brawling." *USA Today*, May 6, 1994, p. 6C.

Bohm, David and Renee Weber. "The Enfolding-Unfolding Universe: A Conversation with David Bohm." In *The Holographic Paradigm and Other Paradoxes*, Ken Wilber, ed. Boulder, CO: Shambhala Publications, 1982.

Brady, Erik. "Survey: Sports Foster Racial Unity." *USA Today*, November 8, 1993.

Branscombe, Nyle R. and Daniel L. Wann. "Physiological Arousal and Reactions to Outgroup Members during Competitions that Implicate an Important Social Identity." *Aggressive Behavior*, v. 18, n. 2, pp. 85-94.

Bronowski, Jacob. *The Ascent of Man*. Boston: Little, Brown, 1971.

Buckley, Steve. "Punishment without Crime." *Sport*. February 1992, p. 24.

Coakley, Jay. *Sport in Society: Issues and Controversies* (second edition). St. Louis: C.V. Mosby Co., 1982.

Coe, Sebastian, David Teasdale, and David Wickham. *More Than a Game: Sport in Our Time*. London: BBC Books, 1992.

Curtis, John. The Mindset for Winning. La Crosse, WI: Coulee Press, 1991.

Dart, Raymond. "The predatory transition from ape to man," in R.E. Leakey, *The Making of Mankind*. New York: E.P. Dutton, 1981.

DeBenedette, Valerie. "Spectator Violence at Sports Events: What Keeps Enthusiastic Fans in Bounds?" *Physician and Sports Medicine*, v. 16, n. 3, March 1988, pp. 202-205, 208, 211.

Dickey, Glenn. *The Jock Empire: Its Rise and Deserved Fall*. Radnor, PA: Chilton Book Company, 1974.

Dychtwald, Ken. "Commentaries on the Holographic Theory: Reflections on the Holographic Paradigm." In *The Holographic Paradigm and Other Paradoxes*, Ken Wilber, ed. Boulder, CO: Shambhala Publications, 1982.

Education Digest. "A Game Plan for Game Safety." *Education Digest*, v. 58, n. 5, January 1993, pp. 52-56.

Eisley, Loren. The Unexpected Universe. New York: Harcourt, Brace, & World, 1969.

Engler, Teri. "Kill 'Em! Sports Violence and the Law." *Update on Law-Related Education*, v. 7, n. 2, Spring 1983, pp. 2-5, 61-63.

ESPN. "Our Violent Games." *Outside the Lines.* Television broadcast, March 23, 1995.

Fain, Gerald S. *Leisure and Ethics: Reflections on the Philosophy of Leisure.* Reston, VA: American Association for Leisure and Recreation, 1991.

Fawcett, Edmund and Tony Thomas. *America and the Americans.* New York: Fontana/Collins, 1982.

Fisher, Millard K. "Problems, Trends, and Dilemmas—What the Future Will Demand and Its Implications for Ethics, Decision-making, and Responsibility for Sports Participation." Paper presented at the Annual Meeting of the American Alliance for Health, Physical Education, Recreation, and Dance. New Orleans, LA, March 29-31, 1990.

Fraleigh, Warren P. "Why the Good Foul Is Not Good." In *Philosophic Inquiry in Sport*, William J. Morgan and Klaus V. Meier, eds. Champaign, IL: Human Kinetics Publishers, 1988.

Galasso, Pasquale J., ed. *Philosophy of Sport and Physical Activity: Issues and Concepts.* Toronto: Canadian Scholars' Press, 1988.

Gallwey, W. Timothy. *The Inner Game of Tennis.* New York: Random House, 1974.

Gallwey, W. Timothy. *Inner Tennis: Playing the Game.* New York: Random House, 1976.

Green, Elmer and Alyce Green. *Beyond Biofeedback.* New York: Delacorte Press, 1977.

Greenberg, Jay. "A Real Spiritual Game." *Sports Illustrated.* March 12, 1990, p. 18.

Greendorfer, Susan L. "Sociology of Sport." *The Physical Educator*, V. 42, n. 4, 1985, pp. 169-174.

Guttmann, Allen. *A Whole New Ball Game: An Interpretation of American Sports.* Chapel Hill, NC: University of North Carolina Press, 1988.

Hanna, Thomas. "Physical Education as Somatic Education." In *Mind and Body: East Meets West*, Seymour Kleinman, ed. Champaign, IL: Human Kinetics Press, 1986.

Harman, Willis W. "The Changing Image of Man/Woman: Signs of a Second Copernican Revolution." In *Mind and Body: East Meets West*, Seymour Kleinman, ed. Champaign, IL: Human Kinetics Press, 1986.

Harris, Harold Arthur. *Greek Athletes and Athletics*. Bloomington, IN: Indiana University Press, 1966.

Harris, Harold Arthur. *Sport in Greece and Rome*. Ithaca NY: Cornell University Press, 1972.

Hellstedt, Jon C. "Kids, Parents, and Sport: Some Questions and Answers." *The Physician and Sports Medicine*, v. 16, n. 4, April 1988, pp. 59-71.

Hendricks, Gay and Jon Carlson. *The Centered Athlete: A Conditioning Program for Your Mind*. Englewood Cliffs, NJ: Prentice-Hall, 1982.

Herrigel, Eugen. *Zen and the Art of Archery*. New York: Vintage, 1971.

Hoch, David. "What Is Sports Law?" *Quest*, V. 37, n. 1, 1985, pp. 60-70.

Homer. *The Iliad*. Robert Fitzgerald, trans. Garden City, NY: Doubleday, 1974.

Horwitz, Tem, Susan Kimmelman, and H.H. Lui. *T'ai Chi Ch'uan: The Technique of Power*. Chicago: Chicago Review Press, 1976.

Huang, Chungliang Al and Jerry Lynch. *Thinking Body, Dancing Mind: Taosports for Extraordinary Performance in Athletics, Business, and Life*. New York: Bantam, 1992.

Hyland, Drew. *Philosophy of Sport*. New York: Paragaon House, 1990.

Hyland, Drew. "Competition and Friendship." *Journal of the Philosophy of Sport*, vol. V, 1978, pp. 27-38.

Isaacs, Neil D. *Jock Culture, U.S.A.: The Takeover of American Life by the Morality of Overemphasized Sports*. New York: W.W. Norton, 1978.

Jenkins, Sally. "Persons Non Grata." *Sports Illustrated*, August 23, 1993, pp. 28-34.

Jerome, John. *The Sweet Spot in Time*. New York: Summit Books, 1980.

Johnson, Chic. "Toward a revisionist philosophy of coaching." In *Mind and Body: East Meets West*, Seymour Kleinman, ed. Champaign, IL: Human Kinetics Publishers, 1986.

Jones, J.C.H., D.G. Ferguson, and K.G. Stewart. "Blood Sports and Cherry Pie: Some Economics of Violence in the National Hockey League," *Economics and Sociology*. January 1993, v. 52, n. 1, p. 63.

Kindred, Dave. "In Need of a Safety Device." *The Sporting News*. December 21, 1992, p. 5.

King, Peter. "Halt the Head-hunting." *Sports Illustrated*. December 19, 1994, pp. 27-30, 37.

Kleinman, Seymour, ed. *Mind and Body: East Meets West*. Champaign, IL: Human Kinetics Press, 1986.

Kretchmer, R. Scott. "Ethics and Sport;." *Journal of the Philosophy of Sport*, v. X, 1983, pp. 21-32.

Kurkjian, Tim. "A Modest Proposal." *Sports Illustrated*. June 18, 1990, p. 53.

Kurkjian, Tim. "New-Age Chin Music." *Sports Illustrated*. June 18, 1990, p. 66.

Lasch, Christopher. "The Degradation of Sport." In *Philosophic Inquiry in Sport*, William J. Morgan and Klaus V. Meier, eds. Champaign, IL: Human Kinetics Publishers, 1988.

Leakey, Richard E. *The Making of Mankind*. New York: E.P. Dutton, 1981.

Leaman, Oliver. "Cheating and Fair Play in Sport." In *Philosophic Inquiry in Sport*, W.J. Morgan and K.V. Meier, eds. Champaign, IL: Human Kinetics Publishers, 1988.

Leonard, George. *The Ultimate Athlete: Re-Visioning Sports, Physical Education and the Body*. New York: Viking, 1974.

Linden, Paul. "The art of aikido: Philosophical education in movement." In *Mind and Body: East Meets West*, Seymour Kleinman, ed. Champaign, IL: Human Kinetics Publishers, 1986.

Loy, John W. and Gerald S. Kenyon. *Sport, Culture, and Society: A Reader on the Sociology of Sport.* New York: Macmillan, 1969.

McCallum, Jack. "Way Out of Control." *Sports Illustrated*, May 23, 1994, pp. 26-31.

McCallum, Jack. "Fight Night at the Palace. *Sports Illustrated.* April 30, 1990, pp. 24-25.

Messner, Michael A. and Donald F. Sabo. *Sex, Violence &Power in Sports: Rethinking Masculinity.* Freedom, CA: The Crossing Press, 1994.

Mihoces, Gary. "'Trash Talk,' Chest-Bumps Fuel the Fire." *USA Today*, May 25, 1994, pp. 1A, 2A.

Ming, Shi and Siao Weijia. *Mind over Matter: Higher Martial Arts.* Berkeley, CA: Frog, Ltd., 1994.

Mitchener, James A. *Sports in America.* New York: Random House, 1976.

Montagu, Ashley, ed. *Learning Non-Aggression: The Experience of Non-Literate Societies.* New York: Oxford University Press, 1978.

Morgan, W.J. and K.V. Meier, eds. *Philosophic Inquiry in Sport.* Champaign, IL: Human Kinetics, 1988.

Morris, Desmond. "Altruistic Behavior," in *Manwatching: A Field Guide to Human Behavior.* New York: Harry Abrams, 1977.

Neilson, Bradley C. "Controlling Sports Violence." *Trial.* June 1990, v. 26, n. 6, pp. 26-31.

Olson, Gregory D. and Norman D. Comfort, III. "Aikido: The art of human movement," in Kleinman, ed., *Mind and Body: East Meets West.* Champaign, IL: Human Kinetics, 1986.

Orlick, Terry. *Winning Through Cooperation.* Washington, D.C.: Acropolis Books, 1978.

Osterhoudt, Robert G. *The Philosophy of Sport: A Collection of Original Essays.* Springfield, IL: Charles C. Thomas, Publisher, 1973.

Patrick, Dick. "The Mind Holds Secrets Beyond the Zone." *USA Today*. March 15, 1994, p. 3C.

Phelps, Teresa Godwin. "Stop Asking Coaches to Pretend." *USA Today*, March 28, 1994, p. 13A.

Phillips, John C. and Walter E. Schafer. "Consequences of Participation in Interscholastic Sports: A Review and Perspectus." In *George Sage, Sport and American Society*, 3rd edition. Reading, MA: Addison-Wesley, 1977.

Plato. *Phaedo*. F.J. Church, trans. New York: Macmillan, 1985.

Plato. *The Republic*. Desmond Lee, trans. New York: Penguin, 1974.

Riesman, David and Reuel Denney. "Football in America: A Study in Cultural Diffusion." In Loy and Kenyon, *Sport, Culture, and Society*. New York: Macmillan, 1969.

Riley, Pat. *The Winner Within: A Life Plan for Team Players*. New York: G.P. Putnam's Sons, 1993.

Roberts, Jane. *The Nature of the Psyche*. Englewood Cliffs, NJ: Prentice-Hall, 1979.

Rosenbloom, Steve. "Fighting Words." *Sport*. January, 1990, pp. 22-26.

Rosenbloom, Steve. "Why Can't the NHL Eliminate Fighting?" *Sport*. October, 1991, p. 81.

Ross, Saul. "Winning and Losing in Sport: A Radical Reassessment." In Galasso, ed. *Philosophy of Sport and Physical Activity*. Toronto: Canadian Scholars' Press, 1988, pp. 56-63.

Sage, George H., ed. *Sport and American Society: Selected Readings*, 3rd edition. Reading, MA: Addison-Wesley, 1980.

Scher, Jon. "Mr. Dirty." *Sports Illustrated*. March 1, 1993, p. 40.

Sherrington, Kevin, "Experts debate the 'dangers' male athletes pose to women." New Britain, CT, *The Day*, October 10, 1994, pp. D1, D8.

Sieh, Ron. *T'ai Chi Ch'uan: The Internal Tradition*. Berkeley, CA: North Atlantic Books, 1992.

Smith, Adam (pseudonym). "Sport Is a Western Yoga." *Psychology Today*, IX (October 1975), pp. 48-51, 74-76.

Smith, Claire. "Behind Brawling: the Pitch Inside." *The New York Times*. June 17, 1993, p. B15.

Sparks, Robert. "Mystical and material: A comparative Analysis." In *Mind and Body: East Meets West*, Seymour Kleinman, ed. Champaign, IL: Human Kinetics Publishers, 1986.

Sperry, Roger. "Some Effects of Disconnecting the Cerebral Hemispheres." *Science*, 217, September 24, 1982, p. 1226.

Stevens, John and Shirata Rinjiro. *Aikido: The Way of Harmony*. Boston: Shambhala, 1984.

Stewart, K.G., Donald G. Ferguson, and J.C.H. Jones. "On Violence in Professional Team Sport as the Endogenous Result of Profit Maximization." *Atlantic Economic Journal*, v. 20, December, 1992, p. 55.

Sullivan, David B. "Commentary and Viewer Perception of Player Hostility: Adding Punch to Televised Sports." *Journal of Broadcasting and Electronic Media*. Fall 1991, v. 35, n. 4, pp. 487-504.

Syer, John and Christopher Connolly. *Sporting Body, Sporting Mind*. New York: Cambridge University Press, 1984.

Talbot, Michael. *The Holographic Universe*. New York: The HarperCollins, 1991.

Taylor, Phil. "Bruise News." *Sports Illustrated*. February 11, 1991, pp. 186-187.

Telander, Rick. *The Hundred Yard Lie*. New York: Simon & Schuster, 1989.

Terry, Peter C. and John J. Jackson. "The Determinants and Control of Violence in Sport." *Quest*, v. 37, n. 1, 1985, pp. 27-37.

Tutko, Thomas and William Bruns. *Winning Is Everything and Other American Myths*. New York: Macmillan, 1976.

Twain, Mark. *A Connecticut Yankee in King Arthur's Court*. New York: Penguin, 1963.

Underwood, John. *Spoiled Sport: A Fan's Notes on the Troubles of Spectator Sports*. Boston: Little, Brown and Company, 1984.

Valenti, John and Ron Naclerio. *Swee' Pea and Other Playground Legends: Tales of Drugs, Violence, and Basketball*. New York: Michael Kesend, 1990.

Vanderzwaag, Harold J. *Toward a Philosophy of Sport*. Reading, MA: Addison-Wesley, 1972.

Vecsey, George. "Basketball Hulksters Concentrate on Business." *The New York Times*, May 16, 1994, p. C4.

Vecsey, George. "First Off, Calm Down Noise and Mascots." *The New York Times*, February 12, 1995, p. 2S.

Vega, Eichard. "Football Minus Frills—and Drills." *USA Weekend*, October 29-31, 1993, p. 8.

Watson, Scott B. "Is there more to practice than the pursuit of perfection?" In *Mind and Body: East Meets West*, Seymour Kleinman, ed. Champaign, IL: Human Kinetics Publishers, 1986.

Watts, Alan. *The Way of Zen*. New York: Pantheon, 1957.

Weisman, Jacob. "Pro Football: the Maiming Game." *The Nation*. January 27, 1992, pp. 84-86.

Weiss, Paul. *Sport: A Philosophic Inquiry*. Carbondale, IL: Southern Illinois University Press, 1969.

Wertz, Spencer K. *Talking a Good Game: Inquiries into the Principles of Sport*. Dallas: Southern Methodist University Press, 1991.

Wigge, Larry. "The All-Stars Who Are Too Good to Be Goons." *The Sporting News*. January 28, 1991, p. 34.

Wigge, Larry. "The 1-2 Punch Against Fighting," *The Sporting News*. September 2, 1991, p. 37.

Wilber, Ken, ed. *The Holographic Paradigm and Other Paradoxes*. Boulder, CO: Shambhala Publications, 1982.

Wulf, Steve. "Basebrawl." *Sports Illustrated.* August 16, 1993, p. 12.

Wulf, Steve. "Brawlgame!' *Sports Illustrated.* August 27, 1990, p. 12.

Ziegler, Earle F. *Sport and Physical Education Philosophy.* Dubuque, IO: Brown and Benchmark, 1989.

Ziegler, Earle F. *Physical Education and Sport Philosophy.* Englewood Cliffs, NJ: Prentice-Hall, 1977.

Ziegler, Earle F. *Problems in the History and Philosophy of Physical Education and Sport.* Englewood Cliffs, NJ: Prentice-Hall, 1968.

Subject Index

Name Index